THE PURE INTENTION

OTHER TITLES BY IBN ʿAṬĀʾ ALLĀH AL-ISKANDARĪ
PUBLISHED BY THE ISLAMIC TEXTS SOCIETY

The Key to Salvation: A Sufi Manual of Invocation

RELATED TITLES

The Qurʾān and the Prophet in the Writings of Shaykh Aḥmad al-ʿAlawī

A Sufi Saint of the Twentieth Century: Shaikh Aḥmad al-Alawī, His Spiritual Heritage and Legacy

The Way of Abū Madyan: The Works of Abū Madyan Shuʿayb

Ibn ʿAṭāʾ Allāh al-Iskandarī

THE PURE INTENTION:

ON KNOWLEDGE OF THE UNIQUE NAME

Al-Qaṣd al-Mujarrad fī Maʿrifat al-Ism al-Mufrad

Translated by Khalid Williams

THE ISLAMIC TEXTS SOCIETY

This first edition published 2018 by
The Islamic Texts Society
Miller's House
Kings Mill Lane
Great Shelford
Cambridge CB22 5EN
United Kingdom
www.its.org.uk

British Library Cataloguing-in-Publication Data.
A catalogue record for this book is available from the British Library.

ISBN: 978 1911141 37 2 paper

Printed and bound in the UK by TJ Books, Padstow, PL28 8RW.

Front cover Arabic calligraphy by Arabiccalligraphy4you.

CONTENTS

Translator's Introduction
VII

THE PURE INTENTION:
ON KNOWLEDGE OF THE UNIQUE NAME

Introduction
I

PART ONE:

Concerning the Lexical Derivation of the Name *Allāh* and Its Parts, Its Separate Letters, How Its Parts Are Interrelated and What They Signify
5

PART TWO:

On the Knowledge of the Perfection and Nobility of the Name *Allāh*, and an Explanation of Its Mysteries and the Unique Benefits of Invoking It, by God's Power
57

TRANSLATOR'S INTRODUCTION

Tāj al-Dīn Abū al-Faḍl Aḥmad ibn Muḥammad ibn ʿAṭā' Allāh al-Iskandarī was born in Alexandria around 658/1259. He was educated in Islamic Law and the Arabic language from an early age, eventually rising to teaching positions at both the Azhar mosque and the Manṣūriyya school in Cairo. After initially harbouring some suspicion towards Sufism, his mind was changed upon meeting Shaykh Abū al-ʿAbbās al-Mursī, the successor to Abū al-Ḥasan al-Shādhilī the founder of the Shādhilī order. As he recounts in his *Laṭā'if al-Minan*, he first sought to visit the Shaykh in 674/1286 after quarrelling with one of disciples, but upon meeting the master in person he was instantly struck with his obvious saintly character and became his most faithful disciple. He served his master until the latter's death in 686/1288, whereupon he succeeded him as head of the Shādhilī order. He continued to teach at the Azhar and Manṣūriyya, as well as instructing his disciples, until his death in Cairo in 709/1309.

Aside from his teaching roles and duties to the order, Ibn ʿAṭā' Allāh was a prolific author. Of those of his works that have reached us, the earliest and by far the best known and most popular is the *Kitāb al-Ḥikam*, a collection of aphorisms on the spiritual path that has come to be considered perhaps the most essential manual of the Sufi path, inspiring dozens if not hundreds of commentaries. His other works include *Kitāb al-Tanwīr fī Isqāṭ al-Tadbīr* on the importance of reliance on God in the Sufi path, *Miftāḥ al-Falāḥ* on the principles of the Shādhilī path and the method of invocation,[1] and *Laṭā'if al-Minan*, a biography of his master Abū al-ʿAbbās al-Mursī and the latter's own master Abū al-Ḥasan al-Shādhilī.

1 Translated by Mary Ann Koury Danner as *The Key to Salvation: A Sufi Manual of Invocation* (Islamic Texts Society, Cambridge, 1996).

No date is known for the composition of *al-Qaṣd al-Mujarrad fī Maʿrifat al-Ism al-Mufrad*, but it was likely one of Ibn ʿAṭāʾ Allāh's later works. This treatise on invocation in general, and invocation of the divine Name *Allāh* in particular, is divided into two parts. Part One looks at the Name itself—its lexical derivation and the question of whether it was derived or not, and its letters and their meanings. The author discusses the divine Names and the Sufi concept of emulating them—being forgiving like the Forgiving, patient like the Patient, strong like the Strong, and so on. However, the author cautions, this is only a figure of speech and the resemblance can only be partial and incomplete, because of the impassable gulf between the transcendence and infinite perfection of God and the contingence and imperfection of man:

> …Such expressions should always be accompanied by a firm affirmation of the divine transcendence and a resolve to overcome one's passions and desires, and to ascend beyond one's base caprice and shed one's bad qualities and replace them with sublime ones, even as a snake sheds its skin and leaves it behind entirely, until there is no room in the heart for anything but God. There is a great difference between 'it is the same as it,' and 'it is like it'.

The author then conducts a more detailed examination of the letters *alif, lām, lām, hāʾ* that form the divine Name *Allāh*, and their meanings and symbolic significance both independently and in relation to one another. He notes how the meaning of the Name is retained even if the letters are successively removed: removing the *alif* leaves *lillāh*, 'to God'; removing the first *lām* leaves *lahū*, 'to Him'; and removing all but the final *hāʾ* still leaves *Hū*, 'He'. Part One ends with an affirmation that *Allāh* is the greatest of all the Names, containing and enveloping all the other divine Names and Qualities:

> It is the Supreme Name, the Name of Godhood by which all created beings were ordained, and by which the earth was spread out and the heavens lifted.

Part Two turns to the more practical matter of the role of invocation (*dhikr*)—invocation of God in general, and of the Name *Allāh* specifically. With reference to the Qur'ān and Sunna, the author discusses the virtue of invocation and establishes that it is the supreme act of worship. He argues that the invocation of the Name *Allāh* is the supreme invocation, because *Allāh* is the Supreme Name. He then discusses the modes and degrees of this invocation, and the differing levels of realisation that the invoker may attain. For Ibn ʿAṭā' Allāh, at its highest level the invocation of the Name is a participation in God's own eternal remembrance of Himself:

> In reality, no one invokes God but God, and no one knows Him but He, and no one truly affirms His Oneness but He.

By emulating the Qualities of God as expressed in His Names, and invoking His Supreme Name with awareness of its meaning and significance, the Sufi can cleanse his heart and fill it with *tawḥīd* until it becomes a worthy abode for God, as the sacred tradition says: 'Neither My Throne nor My Footstool can contain Me, but the heart of My servant can.'

The invocation of the Divine Name *Allāh* has a central importance in several Sufi orders, particularly the Shādhilī order of the author where it is considered the highest rank of invocation, permitted to disciples only when the master deems them qualified. This has become a defining characteristic of the order—particularly in the branches tracing back to the great Moroccan reviver of the school Moulay al-ʿArabī al-Darqāwī (d. 1238/1823)—the masters of which are often known by the epithet 'renowned for the transmission of the Supreme Name', signifying that they are qualified to teach the method of this invocation to their disciples. Moulay al-ʿArabī wrote:

We believe, and God knows best, that spiritual annihilation (*fanāʾ*) can be attained swiftly, God willing, by a certain method of invoking the Name of Majesty *Allāh*. I found this method described by the eminent master and saint of God Sidi Abū al-Ḥasan al-Shādhilī, may God be pleased with him, in a book in the possession of one of the jurists of our brethren the Banū Zarwāl, may God protect them from all error. It was also taught to me by my noble master and guide Abū al-Ḥasan Sidi ʿAlī [al-Jamal], may God be pleased with him, but in a method that is even swifter and sounder. It is to imagine the five letters of the Name as one says *Allāh, Allāh, Allāh*, and whenever they should slip from one's mind to quickly call them back, even if one should have to recall them a thousand times a night and a thousand times a day. This method produced a tremendous contemplative state in me, such that in the beginning when I followed it for over a month it presented me with all manner of gifts of knowledge—but these I ignored, focusing solely on the invocation of the Name and imagining its letters, until after a month I was visited by God's words, *He is the First and the Last, the Outwardly Manifest and the Inwardly Hidden* (Q.LVII.3). At first, I attempted to move past them and carry on with my work, as I always would, but this time they would not leave me alone. They overpowered me and refused to permit me to move past them, despite my best efforts to resist them. Eventually when I saw that they would never leave me be I said to them, 'I understand His words *He is the First and the Last … and the Inwardly Hidden*, but I cannot understand what He means by *the Outwardly Manifest*, since the only things we see outwardly are the works of His creation.' To this they replied, 'If He had meant anything by *the Outwardly Manifest* other than what you see outwardly, He would have

> been speaking about what is hidden, not what is manifest. Yet I say to you: *the Outwardly Manifest.*' It was then that I understood that nothing exists but God, and that there is no being but Him. Praise be to God, and thanks be to God![1]

Moulay al-ʿArabī is describing the Sufi doctrine of the 'oneness of being' (*waḥdat al-wujūd*), most commonly associated with Ibn ʿArabī but found whether in name or in principle in the writings of many masters, including our author Ibn ʿAṭā' Allāh who meditated on it at length in his *Ḥikam*. For such masters, the invocation of the Name *Allāh* represents a distillation of the essence of both doctrine and praxis, which explains its supreme importance in the order. Just as Ibn ʿAṭā' Allāh describes how the removal of each letter of the divine Name still leaves something significant behind so that even when only the final letter is left the essential meaning is still retained, one could say the same about the place of the *dhikr* of the Supreme Name in Sufi doctrine and practice; even if all else were lost, the essence would remain. In his defence of this *dhikr* against the criticisms of certain opponents of Sufism in his homeland, the Algerian Shādhilī master Aḥmad al-ʿAlawī (d. 1934) wrote:

> Remembrance [*dhikr*] is the mightiest rule of the religion ... The law was not enjoined upon us, neither were the rites of worship ordained but for the sake of establishing the remembrance of God ... In a word, our performance of the rites of worship is considered strong or weak according to the degree of our remembrance of God while performing them.[2]

۞ ۞ ۞

1 Moulay al-ʿArabī al-Darqāwī, *Rasā'il* (Dār al-Kutub al-ʿIlymiyya, Beirut, 2003), Epistle 13, p. 45.

2 Martin Lings, *A Sufi Saint of the Twentieth Century* (Islamic Texts Society, Cambridge, 1993), pp. 96, 97.

This translation of *al-Qaṣd al-Mujarrad fī Maʿrifat al-Ism al-Mufrad* is based on two editions of the *Qaṣd*, that of Dār al-Kutub al-ʿIlmiyya (Beirut 2002), and that of the Maktaba Madbūlī (Cairo, 2001). Some passages from it were previously translated by Khalid Williams in the Mabda English Monograph Series, No. 23, 'On Invoking the Divine Name "Allah"' (Royal Aal al-Bayt Institute for Islamic Thought, 2012).

NOTE ON THE DIVISIONS WITHIN THE TRANSLATION AND ON CAPITALISATION

The Pure Intention: On Knowledge of the Unique Name is one of the most profound works ever written on the subject of Divine Unity or *tawḥīd* and the divine Name *Allāh*. This short treatise can be compared to an intricate tapestry of the subject and demands deep reflection so as to take in the sublime truths that it reveals. The work was written in two parts; however, it was decided to insert dividers in the text wherever Ibn ʿAṭā' Allāh introduced new ideas. The text itself naturally allowed this as it is interspersed with numerous poems which Ibn Aṭā' Allāh used to sum up points. In addition, in places the author gives direct instructions to the reader, such as, 'Know that…', and these too have been used to divide the text. The translator and publisher hope that these divisions will be of help to readers tackling the, at times, challenging metaphysics of the work, and will allow readers to gain more from what they read.

A decision was also made regarding the capitalisation of the divine Names and Qualities in order to make the text as clear as possible and in order to prevent confusion. Wherever possible capital letters have been retained, for example, in the plurals Names and Qualities. However, Name has been used exclusively for the Name *Allāh*, while 'a name' or 'the name *al-Ṣamad*' is in lower case. Wherever It and Its have been used, this indicates the divine Essence. We understand that this is an unsatisfactory compromise, and ask forgiveness of the All-Merciful.

THE PURE INTENTION:

ON KNOWLEDGE OF THE UNIQUE NAME

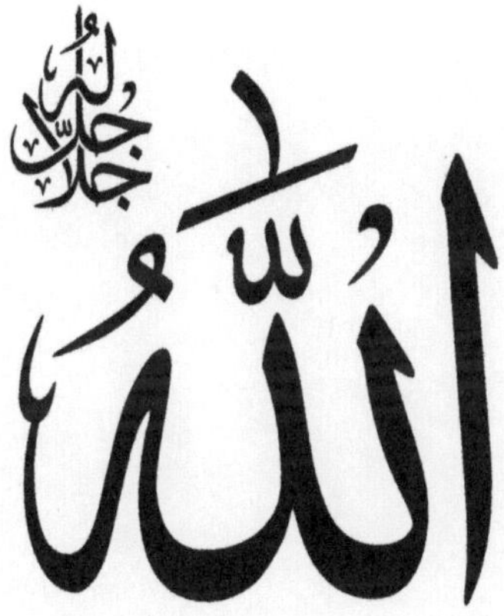

INTRODUCTION

Praise be to God, who illuminated the hearts of His saints with the lights of His guidance. He purified their inner secrets for the manifestation of His majesty, beauty and perfect might. He selected them to remain ever close to Him, in proximity to His presence. He prepared them and chose them for His intimate discourse and conversation. He informed them and taught them the truths of the secret of His lordship's Names, and manifested Himself to them through His Names and Qualities, so that the radiant sun of His gnosis shone upon them. He wiped their souls clean of all coloration,[1] and bathed their hearts in the brilliant light of His Uniqueness. Thus, did He impart unto them understanding and inspiration, and taught them the proper etiquettes of keeping His company. Then He revealed to them the beauty, perfection and splendour of His noble countenance, and turned His full attention to them. He showed them the wonders of His creation, the splendours of His deeds and the glories of His wisdom. They bore witness to the marvels of His kingdom, His dominion and His domination, and then, transfixed by their vision of Him, they became oblivious and heedless of them. Then He gave them strength and made them subsist through Him, and comforted them with the delicate kindness of His mercy. He drew them closer to Himself through His benevolence and kindness, and bestowed upon them His grace, and gave them to drink from the wine of His love. He vouchsafed to them His secrets and gifted to them His treasures.

All this He did, and He made the foundation and the root of it all knowledge of the Name of his Godhood [*Allāh*], in which He hid His secret from all those from whom He willed to conceal it,

1 Literally, 'all their colouring/colours' (*talwīnihā*); meaning any expressions of separative individuality.

veiling them with certain outward forms and manifold meanings. The beginning of understanding it is in its first *alif*, and the end of knowledge of it is in the meaning of its final *hā'*.[1] Fortunate indeed is the one for whom the veils of its impenetrable outer meaning are lifted, uncovering the light of the inner meaning so that he may pluck its secret fruit, breathe in its fragrant aroma and taste its delicious sweetness. Through it, he comes to know and bear witness to its outer markers and its inner signposts in existence, and its heights and its depths, according to the nature of His Essence and the reality of His Substance. He is then permitted to partake in His dominion over creation through the command of 'Be!',[2] thereby bringing things into existence in accordance with his will. Let all praise be to God as befits His majesty, for all the outward and inward favours He has showered upon us!

We bear witness before God to His true oneness and absolute unity. There is no god but He, One in His being, Magnificent in His qualities, Almighty in His Uniqueness. We bear witness also to His prophet and messenger—to his perfect prophethood, universal message, and special servitude—Muḥammad, may God bless him and his family, wives, children, descendants and household. May God be pleased with all his Companions, and all the folk of his community and faith who followed in their virtuous footsteps.

To proceed: the elixir of increase, the alchemy of happiness, foundation for every foothold, state and station, and the deepest root of all spiritual excellence (*iḥsān*), faith (*īmān*) and submission to God (*islām*), is knowledge of the divine Oneness (*tawḥīd*). This knowledge is unfettered by intrusive restrictions, and protected from the designs of blind rote learning. It is known as the science of the divine Names and Qualities (*ʿilm al-asmā' wa'l-ṣifāt*), which is an

1 The Arabic divine Name *Allāh* is spelt ALLH, or *alif-lām-lām-hā'* to give the letters their full names.

2 *When He decrees something, He but says to it, 'Be!', and it is* (Q.II.117). Ibn ʿAṭā' Allāh may be alluding here to the *ḥadīth qudsī*: 'Obey Me, O my servant, and I will make you lordly (*rabbāniyyan*); you will say to a thing "Be!" and it will be.'

ancient science that cannot be marred by unnecessary innovation. It is the culmination of all the discourse of the meanings of the divine Name,[1] and the sum of all metaphysical secrets and subtleties. It is a collection of the most precious treasures and the most valuable hidden gems. It is the source of all religious knowledge, and the locus of all gnosis and certitude. Every science is as noble as its subject, and every knower is as noble as his knowledge; and there is nothing nobler than the Real and seeking It. Nothing in this world is nobler than knowledge of God and nearness to Him, and nothing in Paradise is nobler than to behold His countenance. Every science depends on its subject and draws its nobility from it, and the science of divine Oneness depends on knowledge of the One (*al-Wāḥid*) and His quality of Oneness (*waḥdāniyya*). Knowledge of God is the highest goal, the most precious pearl, and a sweet draught for everyone who drinks it, and they can only enjoy a draught of it one by one.[2] It is the thing that is sought out for its own sake, and is a font of constant increase. The greatest of states and most perfect of blessings are attained through it. The wayfarer's first step is the search for gnosis, and his final destination is the Oneness of Essence and Attribute, because the knowledge of God is the ultimate goal and His Oneness is the finest and most perfect end. Knowledge of it gives the invoker inner understanding and realisation. Acting in accordance with it increases the wayfarer in conviction and grace. When someone attains the noblest and highest of sciences and wisdoms, and the finest, most profound and most beneficial meanings, and gains understanding of their inner realities and knowledge of their outward appearances and mysteries, his inner heart takes on its true substance and his outward comportment becomes refined, and only then can he truly be called a human being. Such a person has truly witnessed the Real, and his attributes and qualities have thus attained essential goodness. He has come to know God through

1 The divine Name, or simply the Name, both in this text and in the wider context of Islamic and Sufi discourse, always refers to the Name *Allāh*.

2 That is, the master and then the disciple.

faith (*īmān*) and certitude (*yaqīn*), and recognised His creation with understanding and discernment.

...In this book,[1] the author related wondrous subtleties and marvellous matters of knowledge and spiritual teachings, rarities, wisdoms and unique insights, which stand on their own and need no further introduction. He called it *The Pure Intention: On Knowledge of the Unique Name* (*al-Qaṣd al-Mujarrad fī Maʿrifat al-Ism al-Mufrad*), by which he meant the Name *Allāh*, glorious and majestic is He! He divided the book into two parts with their own themes, and provided for each of them authentic attestations and sound proofs from the Qur'ān, the Sunna and the teachings of the enlightened scholars, the renowned folk of virtue and the Sufis. God alone grants the grace to lead us to what is right, and protect us from what is harmful.

1 A passage is omitted here from both the Cairo and Beirut editions; apparently the remainder of the author's introduction was lost, and a later copyist added a few words about the book to serve as a replacement.

PART ONE

Concerning the Lexical Derivation of the Name *Allāh* and Its Parts, Its Separate Letters, How Its Parts are Interrelated and What They Signify

God says, *Allāh!*[1] *There is no god but He, the Living, the All-Sustaining!*[2] *Allāh! There is no god but He, and He shall certainly gather you on the Day of Resurrection, in which there is no doubt. Who is truer in speech than Allāh?*[3] *Allāh! There is no god but He, the Lord of the Mighty Throne!*[4] *Your god is none but Allāh, besides whom there is no other god. In His knowledge, He encompasses all things.*[5] *He is Allāh in the heavens and on earth. He knows what you conceal and what you reveal, and He knows what you acquire.*[6] *Truly I am Allāh! There is no god but I, so worship Me.*[7]

Consider, may God aid you, how in these verses and others like them He begins by stating the Name *Allāh*, putting aside all others and affirming it. If He manifests any of His other Names, they are attributes and qualities of this one Name. If He manifests it with the letter *hā'*,[8] then it refers back to Him, it comes from Him and returns to Him, for He can only be mentioned if the *hā'* is manifested. This will be discussed later, as will all the letters of the Name, God willing.

1 Throughout this translation, *Allāh* has been retained when the author's intention is to emphasise the Name *Allāh* as opposed to other Names; otherwise *Allāh* has been translated as 'God'.

2 Q.II.255.

3 Q.IV.87.

4 Q.XXVII.26.

5 Q.XX.98.

6 Q.VI.3.

7 Q.XX.14.

8 The letter *hā'* is the last letter of *Allāh* and also represents the pronoun *hū*, meaning 'He'.

His words *He is Allāh in the heavens and on earth* are akin to His words *It is He who in heaven is God* (ilāh) *and on earth is God.*[1] That is, His divinity, His worship, His remembrance, His actions, His wisdom and His command are recognised in heaven and earth.

The Prophet, may God bless him and grant him peace, said, 'I have been commanded to fight these people[2] until they say that there is no god but God (*lā ilāha illā Allāh*),' and in another narration, 'until they testify that there is no god but God, and believe in me and in what I have brought. If they do so, their lives and possessions will be safe from me, except for the rights of the law, and their reckoning will fall to God.'

He also said, may peace be upon him, to Muʿādh b. Jabal, 'O Muʿādh, if any person testifies that there is no god but God and that Muḥammad is the Messenger of God, God will protect him from Hell.' Muʿādh said, 'O Messenger of God, should I not tell the people of this so they may rejoice?' He replied, 'If you do, they will rely on it.'

He also said, may peace be upon him, 'The best thing I and the prophets before me ever said is, "There is no god but God, alone without partner."'

He also said, may peace be upon him, to Abū Hurayra, 'If you ever meet someone who testifies that there is no god but God with total certitude in his heart, give him glad tidings of Paradise.'

۞ ۞ ۞

Consider, may God give you success, that God and His Messenger have linked knowledge (*ʿilm*) with divine Oneness (*tawḥīd*) and worship (*ʿibāda*) with gnosis (*maʿrifa*). God says, *Know that there is no god but God.*[3] The Prophet said, 'Anyone who dies while knowing that there is no god but God will enter Paradise.' Another narration has, 'Anyone who dies while testifying'; testimony means knowledge, as

1 Q.XLIII.84.
2 Quraysh, with whom he was at war.
3 Q.XLVII.19.

in God's words *We did not testify, nor did we know.*[1] God also says, *I created the jinn and mankind only that they might worship Me;*[2] that is, 'that they might know Me.'

When the Prophet, peace be upon him, sent Muᶜādh b. Jabal to Yemen, he said to him, 'You are going to people who follow the Book, so let the first thing to which you invite them be worship of God. If they acknowledge God, tell them that God has charged them with certain obligations.' So, he based the necessity for knowledge of the obligations on the prior necessity of knowledge of God's Oneness.

All the prophets, may peace be upon them, were united in guiding mankind to knowledge of the divine Oneness. God says, *We never sent a messenger before you save that We revealed to him, 'There is no god but I, so worship Me.'*[3] The Prophet, peace be upon him, said, 'The best thing I and the prophets before me ever said is, "There is no god but God, alone without partner."' There was no difference among the prophets when it came to the divine Oneness; only their laws differed. *To each of you We gave a law and a way.*[4]

'There is no god but God' delivers the created soul from immediate torment in the present, and from the greater torment of the Hereafter. Submission to God (*islām*)[5] is founded on its utterance; faith (*īmān*) is founded on its principles and practice; spiritual excellence (*iḥsān*) is founded on the understanding of its doctrines and how to bring them together; and through recognition of its nobility, the soul ascends to the principles of certitude (*īqān*). Thus, uttering it is submission to

1 Q.XII.81.
2 Q.LI.56.
3 Q.XXI.25.
4 Q.V.48.
5 In this sentence, Ibn ᶜAṭā' Allāh is alluding to the well-known *ḥadīth* of Gabriel. In the *ḥadīth*, Gabriel comes to the Prophet in the shape of a man and asks the Prophet, in the presence of his Companions, to define *islām*, *īmān* and *iḥsān*. The first part of the sentence can also be translated as 'The religion of Islam is founded on the utterance of this creed.'

God, implementing it is faith, understanding it is spiritual excellence, and realising it is certitude.

۞ ۞ ۞

The outward meaning [of 'there is no god but God'] is the first step on the road to felicity. Its outward meaning in the world of the Kingdom (*al-Mulk*) is the beginning of spiritual witnessing (*shahāda*); its inner meaning is the understanding of its purpose in the world of the Dominion (*al-Malakūt*), paving the way for gnosis (*maʿrifa*); and its true reality is the unveiling of its secrets in the world of Domination (*al-Jabarūt*), the final end of spiritual witnessing.

In this life, it bounds the heart to the implications of faith; in the Hereafter, it leads to the unveiling and direct witnessing of the implications of certitude. In this life, it secures protection for life and property;[1] in the Hereafter, it secures the soul's salvation. If someone says, 'There is no god but God, and Muḥammad is the Messenger of God,' his life and property are protected except for legal penalties. Anyone who dies while knowing that there is no god but God and Muḥammad is the Messenger of God will enter Paradise.

۞ ۞ ۞

['There is no god but God'] encompasses the secrets of the meaning of divine Oneness (*tawḥīd*), the gnosis of divine Uniqueness (*tafrīd*), and the understanding of detachment from all but the Divine (*tajrīd*). It proves the truth of the Prophet's words, 'I was gifted with succinct speech (*jawāmiʿ al-kalim*).' If someone seeks God through his own means without following the right channel, his *tawḥīd* will not be sound and he will be turned back. If someone seeks God through God and His Messenger, which is the path of knowledge, his *tawḥīd* will be sound and he will be guided. The one

1 The life and property of Muslims are protected under Islamic Law. Therefore, the life and property of anyone who becomes a Muslim by saying 'There is no god but God and Muḥammad is His messenger' are protected.

who knows God through faith will obey Him; the one who knows Him through certitude will prefer Him over everything else; the one who knows him through *tawḥīd* will glorify Him. The one who does not attain gnosis through knowledge of God and His qualities, and through increasing understanding of the reality of His *tawḥīd*, is veiled; and the veiled one is lost. The faith of the knowledgeable results from certitude. The Messenger of God, may God bless him and grant him peace, said, 'Certitude is all of faith.' Studying the traditions and narrations about the science of faith is stronger and more beneficial than blindly following the faith of another; and direct unveiling and innate understanding of the science of *tawḥīd* is better and stronger still.

So 'there is not god but God, Muḥammad is the messenger of God' is essential for humanity: to believe it in the heart, and profess it with the tongue, and be true to it in the mind. If faith rests only in the shell of a person's heart, then he will love this world and the Hereafter alike. If faith reaches the inner part of his heart, he will scorn this world and love the Hereafter, and he will disobey his caprices (*hawā*). If faith penetrates to the deepest regions of his heart, then he will turn away from everything besides God.

Tawḥīd is knowledge, and knowledge is the root of faith, and faith is belief. When the heart believes something, this is called knowledge; and when this knowledge strengthens, it is called certitude; and when it strengthens further still, it is called *tawḥīd*; and when it becomes as firm as a mountain, it is called gnosis (*maʿrifa*). The one who comes to know the inner doctrines of submission to God is like the one who discovers a treasure; the one who comes to know the inner doctrines of faith is like the one who discovers a gold mine; and the one who comes to know the deepest secrets of spiritual excellence is like the one who discovers alchemy. In the firmament of felicity, the planet is submission to God, the atmosphere is faith, the moon is spiritual excellence, and the sun is certitude.

'There is no god but God' is a statement composed of negation and affirmation. The negation denies all the attributes of temporality (*ḥudūth*), deficiency (*naqṣ*) and nonbeing (*ʿadam*); and the affirmation confirms the attributes of transcendence (*tanzīh*), perfection (*kamāl*) and eternality (*qidam*). The one who beholds the existence of the Real through the eye of eternity, and beholds all else besides Him through the eye of temporality and nonbeing, will witness His eternality and will say, 'I have never seen anything without seeing God before it.' The one who beholds Him through the eye of subsistence (*baqā'*), and beholds His creation through the eye of extinction (*fanā'*), will witness the secret of His eternality and will say, 'I have never seen anything without seeing God after it.' The one who beholds Him through the eye of knowledge (*ʿilm*) and power (*qudra*), and beholds His creation through the eye [that sees it] ignorance, incapacity and weakness, will witness His action and His domination and will say, 'I have never seen anything without seeing God with it.'

۞ ۞ ۞

The basis of witnessing (*mushāhada*) can be divided into three categories: witnessing a deed through a deed (*fiʿl bi-fiʿl*), witnessing a quality through a quality (*ṣifa bi-ṣifa*), and witnessing an essence through an essence (*dhāt bi-dhāt*). The one who beholds the Real through the Real will see all the divine Names and Qualities manifested before him and see how they flow through all things, and how the divine knowledge flows through all knowable things. The one who beholds things through knowledge will see how the divine design is manifested in all that is created, and how the divine actions are manifested in all that is acted upon. And when a person beholds through God, not through his own self, all causal connections will be severed, and all created things will disappear, and all expressions and indications will melt away. A poet said,

> I see Him in everything I see;
> I call Him in secret in my heart, and He responds.

With Him I have filled my heart, my hearing, my sight,
My all, my parts, so how could He ever be absent?

Know that *tawḥīd* means to affirm the eternality and uniqueness of the Maker, and to negate all nonbeing. Now, knowledge of the divine Uniqueness requires acknowledgement of the uniqueness of the Name [*Allāh*], while attaining detachment from all besides God requires knowledge of His transcendence. The foundation of 'there is no god but God' is affirmation of the Name of Godhood (*ulūhiyya*) and His complete Uniqueness, the denial of godhood to aught but Him, and the recognition of His transcendence beyond all opposites and counterparts. When the meaning and mystery of this is understood, submission to God (*islām*) becomes sound; by testifying to it, faith (*īmān*) becomes complete and spiritual excellence (*iḥsān*) is perfected.

Now, dear reader, with the help of God I will explain to you the meanings and qualities of this Unique Name [*Allāh*], the secrets of its letters—both combined and separate from each other—such that anyone who comprehends them will be illuminated in a way that is commensurate with his capacity to understand, as well as his level of spiritual adeptness. May God strengthen you with the means of increase and give you understanding of the mysteries of *tawḥīd*, by His grace.

Know that this Name, this unique, glorious, precedential, singular Name—the Name *Allāh*—is the Name of the Supreme Essence, which is endowed with the attributes of Divinity, Lordship, Oneness, Uniqueness and Plenitude, transcendentally removed from modality and comparability, and too holy to be encompassed in knowledge by the human mind. *Allāh*: it is the Name of God, the One, the Eternal, the Living, the Sustaining, the Sublime, the Infinite, the Permanent, the Timeless, the Great, the Transcendent, the Absolute, the Beyond-Time who remains ever First and Last, Outwardly Manifest and Inwardly Hidden, the Sole Possessor of True Being, the Necessary Being. Every other being draws its existence from Him, so that it is non-existent in its own right, and existent only by Him who gives it existence.

It is the greatest of all the Names, because it refers to the Supreme Essence, in which is synthesises all the perfection of the divine Qualities. The perfection of the Essence is the perfection of Being and Its timeless and eternal presence, without beginning or end. He can never cease to be; His Being is necessary, as is His Eternality. A poet said,

> Your majesty, O Holy One, is boundless;
> Your holiness is fathomless.
> You are transcendently distinct from all creation;
> Your transcendence is pure and glorious.
> Your decree is inescapable, Your command fulfilled;
> That which You will cannot be repelled.
> Yours is the Supreme Quality, and all who serve you
> Are honoured enough in being called Your servants.

Now the scholars differ as to whether this Unique Name is morphologically derived or not. This question may be approached from three perspectives: that of language (*lugha*), that of wisdom (*ḥikma*), and that of gnosis (*maʿrifa*).

Concerning the first perspective, that of language, there are two opinions. Some say it is morphologically derived and that the source of its derivation is known; others say that we cannot say anything about this, but must accept the Name as it is. The latter group say that it is not permitted to trace the Name's derivation at all, because God says *hal taʿlamu lahū samiyyā*,[1] which can be interpreted in three ways.

1 Q.xix.65. Literally, 'Do you know of any who have His Name?'

Firstly, 'Do you know of anyone besides *Allāh* who is called *Allāh*, or any name for Him other than that which He has given Himself?' Secondly, 'Do you know of anyone who deserves to be described by such perfect Names and Qualities as God does and is?' Thirdly, 'Do you know of any name which is greater than this Supreme Name, or do you imagine it is derived from something else, as human names are? For nothing resembles Him.'

According to this understanding, the Name refers to the Essence of God through which all the Qualities exist; it is like the word *ʿilm*, which simply means 'knowledge' and is not derived from anything else. It is a Name which God Almighty has chosen for Himself alone, by which He denotes His Essence, and which He has given precedence above all the other Names, so that they are all adjectives for it and connected to it. All the other Names are called 'the Names of *Allāh*', and are known by their relationship to this one Name: they are called 'the Names of *Allāh*', not 'the Names of *al-Ṣabūr* (the All-Patient)' or 'the Names of *al-Ghaffār* (the All-Forgiving)' or 'the Names of *al-Jabbār* (the Irresistible)'. One cannot declare oneself a Muslim without mention of this Name and no other Name can be accepted in place of it; one cannot say *lā ilāha illa al-Ghaffār* ('there is no god but the All-Forgiving'), or 'the Merciful', or 'the Irresistible'; one may only say *lā ilāha illa Allāh*. The Qur'ān and *Ḥadīth* also express themselves in this way, because it is the clearest way to refer to the concept of divinity, and means nothing else. It is more recognised as fulfilling this function than any other name, and conveys this concept more clearly and perfectly, needing no other name to clarify it, while all the other Names are known only in connection with it. [God] designated it for speech (*nuṭq*), invocation (*dhikr*) and connection (*taʿalluq*), and excluded attribution (*ittiṣāf*) [to any other] or emulation (*takhalluq*). A poet said,

O you who, by your search and study
Have approached a secret above all ascription,
Take the advice of one who says:

Do not allow for any resemblance
For the Name of God, which is unique
And has no derivation, and is shared by none.
He chose it for Himself, and kept it secret,
Not even disclosing it in the other scriptures.
He made it the Name of His own Essence,
So that the other Names marvelled at it:
By means of them, the Name is praised,
And thanked for blessings, and lauded in speeches.
Proclaim it always, then, and allow for it no precedent,
If you are a person of depth and decorum.

Those who are of the opinion that the Name is indeed morphologically derived say that it is derived from five things: adoration, salvation, veiling, attachment and height. It is said to be derived from adoration (*walah*) in the sense that its origin is *ilāh* (god), and a god is something that is adored, and from whom needs are sought, and from whom protection is asked at times of trial, and whose grace is hoped for, and whose justice is feared. A poet said,

In my times of trial, I look to you to represent me,
And receive from you help which is kind and noble.

This is based on the notion that the Name is derived from the definite article *al-* which was added to *ilāh* by way of implying grandeur, to make *al-ilāh*, 'the God'; the letter *alif* was then removed, and the two *lāms* joined, the *lām* of grandeur joining with the *lām* of glorification, to make *Allāh*. Since *Allāh* is the Name of God, it implies *walah* (which means both 'adoration' and 'grief'), either in the sense of the servant's rapture and joy, or in the sense of his grief and fear, as he passes between the two states of contraction and expansion. In the state of contraction, he feels awe and consequently bewilderment; and in the state of expansion, he feels closeness and consequently joy. The one who knows his Lord seeks refuge in Him, calls out to

Him, adores Him and turns away from all besides Him, preferring His contentment to his own caprice. A poet said,

> May God love those beautiful women who,
> When they saw my worship (*ta'alluh*), praised God
> and turned to Him.[1]

Concerning the Name's derivation from the concept of 'veil', it is based on the word *lāh*, which can mean 'to be veiled'. God is veiled from mankind and hidden from their sight in this world. A poet said,

> She was veiled (*lāhat*), and neither hide nor hair of her was
> ever seen;
> Would that she had come out, so we could have looked
> upon her!

The one who knows his Lord is aware of Him, and monitors his own soul, and knows that He can see him though He cannot be seen, and is shy of Him.

As for the Name's derivation from the concept of 'height', it is also based on the word *lāh*: the sun is said to have *lāhat* when it reaches the zenith, its highest point. Thus, it has been said,

> God is on high (*lāh al-ilāh*) at the highest of heights;
> It is enough for me to know that my deeds ascend to Him.

Now concerning the second perspective, that of wisdom, it has been said that the Almighty Real has designated this Unique Name—*Allāh*—to Himself alone, and barred any other from being named by it, and prevented mankind from claiming it and adopting it, or describing one another by it, because of the greatness and magnificence of divinity. God says, *Allāh: there is no god but He, the Lord of*

1 The line is by Ru'ba b. al-ʿAjjāj, telling the story of how some beautiful women with whom he used to consort were moved by his repentance and new-found piety.

the Mighty Throne;[1] *Is there another god with Allāh? Nay, but most of them have no knowledge;*[2] *Surely you, and that you were serving apart from Allāh, are fuel for Hell; you shall go down to it. If those had been gods, they would never have gone down to it; yet every one of them shall therein abide forever;*[3] *Then exalted be Allāh, the King, the True! There is no god but He, the Lord of the noble Throne. And whosoever calls upon another god with Allāh, whereof he has no proof, his reckoning is with his Lord; surely the unbelievers shall not prosper.*[4] An authentic *ḥadīth* says, 'God Almighty says, "Pride is My garment and greatness is My cloak; and whoso contests Me in either one of them, him I will destroy;"' that is, I will send him to Hell. The divine Name expresses That to which hearts turn in sincere devotion, and That to which bodies and limbs turn in sincere humility of worship. He is the Absolute Necessary Being, and the true Real, and all besides Him are perishing, non-existent and false. The Prophet, may God bless him and grant him peace, said that the truest thing any poet ever said was the words of Labīd,

Verily, all besides God is naught.

Now concerning the third perspective, that of gnosis, it has been said that the Real chose this Name—*Allāh*—for three reasons:

Firstly, for itself, since it is unique and shared by no one, neither metaphorically nor literally, because of the mysteries, wisdoms and meanings it embodies, and because of the uniqueness and glory it implies.

Secondly, because of the subtle meanings and noble qualities it synthesises. Other Names can have one or two meanings, such as Creator, Maker, Designer, Beginner, Cause, and so on, which all

1 Q.xxvii.26.
2 Q.xxvii.61.
3 Q.xxi.98-99.
4 Q.xxiii.116-117.

share the same meaning, even though each one has something that marks it out from the others. Consider also Names such as Provider, Giver of Blessings, Kind, Giver of Grace, Generous and Munificent, all mean essentially the same thing. All the other Names and Qualities might share common meanings with others, or be singular and have only one meaning. The Name *Allāh*, however, has meanings beyond count and limit, and all the other Names ultimately refer back to it and act as adjectives for it, and are defined by it, while it is not defined by anything but the Essence.

Thirdly, because it is distinguished by mysteries which are not present in any of the other Names. God's Grace, Glory, Names and Qualities are all tremendous perfections, but this one Name has an additional perfect distinction which sets it aside from all of them. Just as, although the Torah, Gospel, Psalms and Qur'ān are all the Word of God, He chose the Qur'ān and set it aside from all of them, He likewise chose this one Name from all his Names for special distinction and glory.

One special distinction of the Name is that it is perfect in its letters, complete in its meaning, unique in its mysteries and singular in its quality. Firstly, it is *Allāh*; if the initial *alif* is removed, it leaves *lām-lām-hā*, which spells *lillāh*, 'to God'. If the first *lām* is then removed, this leaves *lām-hā*, which spells *lahū*, 'to Him'. Finally, if the second *lām* is removed, this leaves the letter *hā*, which signifies the third person pronoun *hu*, 'He'. Thus, every letter of the Name has a complete meaning and a perfect distinction, and its meaning does not change. When the letters are separated, no benefit is lost, nor any wisdom removed, and each successive word has a wondrous and marvellous meaning of its own. The meaning of these words and their letters will be explained at the end of this section, God willing.

The other Names are not like this, for if their letters are removed or separated, their meanings change and they are nullified and spoiled, and no longer give any benefit. This shows how this Name is universal and perfect, both in general and in detail. The removal, separation or isolation of its letters does not affect its meanings or blot out any of its mysteries; its parts are not less than its sum.

۞ ۞ ۞

Know that the Most Beautiful Names number one thousand, of which there are three hundred in the Torah, three hundred in the Gospel, three hundred in the Psalms, one in the scriptures of Abraham, and ninety-nine in the Qur'ān. Now the meanings of all these Names are synthesised in the ninety-nine Names of the Qur'ān, which encompass them and contain all of their virtues, mysteries and treasures; and of all the Names in all the scriptures, the first of them is *Allāh*. This is why this Name is the most frequently uttered by people as they go about their affairs: whether it be a word, a deed or anything else, it should be begun with the Name *Allāh*. God says, *He said, 'Embark upon it, and may its course and its berthing be in the Name of Allāh;*[1] *Invoke the Name of Allāh upon it, and be conscious of Allāh; for Allāh is swift in reckoning;*[2] *Eat that over which the Name of Allāh has been invoked;*[3] *Eat not that over which the Name of Allāh has not been invoked, for it is wicked;*[4] *Say not of anything, 'I shall do it on the morrow' without, 'If Allāh so wills';*[5] *O you who believe, remember the favours of Allāh upon you;*[6] *O you who believe, remember Allāh often;*[7] *The remembrance of Allāh is greatest.*[8] All this is an encouragement to invoke this Name. The specifics of its invocation will be discussed in the second part of this epistle, God willing.

Now the first of the Most Beautiful Names and the one with which every *sūra* of the Qur'ān opens is, *In the Name of Allāh, the Compassionate, the Merciful (bi'smi 'Llāh al-Raḥmān al-Raḥīm)*. There is a profound meaning to this being the first of the Names, which is that

1 Q.XI.41.
2 Q.V.4.
3 Q.VI.118.
4 Q.VI.121.
5 Q.XVIII.22-23.
6 Q.V.11.
7 Q.XXXIII.41.
8 Q.XXIX.45.

mercy (*raḥma*) is the first of all things, as an authentic *ḥadīth* says, 'God said, "I am *Allāh*, and there is no god but Me, the Compassionate, the Merciful. My mercy outpaces my wrath."' The two great imams, Mālik b. Anas and Muḥammad b. Idrīs al-Shāfiʿī, may God be pleased with them, explained that although this Name, the Name *Allāh*, is not in it [the *basmala*] in its entirety, it is there partially because it says, 'of God' as though it were *li'llāh* (meaning 'to God' or 'of God') rather than *Allāh*. [Mālik] made a distinction between the Name itself and the possessive *lām*,[1] and said that the divine Name must retain its initial *alif* in order to be complete because the *alif* is the root of the Name and the first thing in it to be counted, and also the first in the term *aḥadiyya* (Oneness), and it is also the first of the letters in general and contains many other secrets, as we shall discuss later, God willing. [Mālik also said] the term 'godhood' refers to what is found in the hearts and bodies of men when they turn to God in worship; He is the worshipped God, to whom is owed both outer and inner worship. Consider how He says, *You do we worship, and Your aid do we seek*;[2] so half of it is godhood, half worship. Shāfiʿī responded that *In the Name of Allāh, the Compassionate, the Merciful* is part of the Mother of the Qur'ān [*sūrat al-Fātiḥa*], and the one who fails to recite it in his prayer renders his prayer flawed and incomplete, or might even have to repeat it.

The one who calls upon God with this Name, calls upon Him with all the thousand Names that are mentioned in all the revealed scriptures. It is permitted for the aspirant (*salik*)[3] to seek to adorn himself with all the other Names and Qualities, except for this Unique Name, which may only be connected to, and not emulated. God

1 The possessive *lām* is the *li* of *li'llāh*.
2 Q.1.5.
3 In Sufi discourse, the initiate is usually called *sālik* (aspirant, literally 'wayfarer'), *murīd* (disciple, literally 'seeker') or *faqīr* (dervish, literally 'pauper'). The word *ṣūfī* is never used in this sense, referring as it does to the perfected Sufi rather than to an individual on the path, although the plural *ṣūfiyya* is often used to refer to the Sufis as a group.

says, *Be you all lordly* (rabbāniyyīn) *active in what you know of the Book;*[1] different canonical readings of this verse read the verb as *what you know*, *what you teach*, and *what you have been taught*. In its substance, knowledge is light and if a person acts on this knowledge, he becomes a being of light in himself and for others. Knowledge is barren, and only becomes fertile when it is implemented. The meaning of 'lordly' (*rabbānī*) is 'one who is adorned with divine qualities', as in the *ḥadīth* of the Prophet, may God bless him and give him peace, 'Adorn yourselves with the qualities of God.' He also said, 'God has one hundred qualities; anyone who adorns himself with even one of them with enter Paradise.'

So, emulating the Names is permitted, and they will become acquired qualities of the aspirant as he follows his path and his spiritual training (*riyāḍa*) and emulates them. Of course, they will not be exactly the same for him, but he will adopt them in the way that the slave adopts the mannerisms of his master. Consider divine Names such as the Forgiving, the Patient, the Coverer, the Merciful, the Generous, the Gracious, the Kind, the Noble, the Relenting, the Just, the Forbearing, and so on. The true distinction of divinity—which is for God and no other—is in the perfection of the Qualities and in the transcendence of the Essence above all change. There can be no comparison between the eternal and the temporal; the qualities of the Real are eternal and transcendent and no human being can truly attain them, for *There is nothing like unto Him,*[2] and nothing resembles him, and nothing can ever be like God. What a human being can attain is something that corresponds to these qualities and can be described with the same words used to describe them, in a general sense but not to the extent of their deeper meanings, nor in the sense of the essence of the qualities being transferred to him. There can be no absolute resemblance to them, nor can they be attained in their true and complete nature. [Moreover] there can be no correspondence between

1 Q.III.79.
2 Q.XLII.11.

them in the way that an object corresponds to the position and shape [of another], nor in the way a substance corresponds to its locus. We only say that it is permitted to emulate them as a very liberal figure of speech, as is common when dealing with matters of resemblance. Yet such expressions should always be accompanied by a firm affirmation of the divine transcendence and a resolve to overcome one's passions and desires, and to ascend beyond one's base caprice and shed one's bad qualities and replace them with sublime ones, even as a snake sheds its skin and leaves it behind entirely, until there is no room in the heart for anything but God. There is a great difference between 'it is the same as it,' and 'it is like it'.

A person can only find felicity and self-realisation by adorning himself with the attributes of God and emulating the meanings of His Names and Qualities as much as is imaginable, until finally the servant becomes lordly; that is, near to the Lord Almighty, and a companion of the Supreme Assembly of pure exalted angels. They are the ones who are near to God, and by emulating their qualities one may become near just as they are; and this, the more one attains their pleasing attributes that made them near to God in the first place. By 'nearness' (*qurb*) here we are speaking of ranks and stations, not places and distances. The more one emulates the angels and adopts their qualities, the further one moves away from the animals and their way of life, and the nearer one approaches the angels and their qualities. Angels are near God, and the one who is near them is also near Him. The greater a person's knowledge and gnosis become, the closer he is to God and the higher he climbs. With this [increase in proximity], more and more truths are revealed to him as they really are, and the details of what he already knows become completely unveiled for him, and he attains clarity and certitude which firmly connect his knowledge to its objects and cause it to subsist and remain sound. Things become perfectly clear to his soul both in this life and the next. When knowledge has total mastery over the objects of its knowledge (*maʿlūm*), this is a kind of perfection which is one of the qualities of lordliness, because of how it encompasses the objects of its knowledge. Once this is achieved, the knowledge will not be at risk of diminishment, dispersal, change or decrease. Such a person will have attained nearness to God. His gnosis will have grown, his insight been illuminated, and his *tawḥīd* will have become firm. This is because God is Eternal and Unending, and is not subject to diminishment, decrease or change, nor are His qualities subject to the vicissitudes that assail created beings. The proximity of the Real to the masses of Muslims (*ʿāma*) is through knowledge and power, to the elite faithful (*khāṣat al-mu'minīn*) through kindness and support, and to the saints (*awliyā'*) and gnostics (*ʿārifūn*) through intimacy and witnessing.

The true nature of nearness to God is to lose the sensation of things from the heart by focusing one's totality on God Almighty. The closest one can come to God is the state of perfecting the soul through the spiritual training of knowledge (*riyāḍat al-ʿilm*) and thereby turning the soul to praiseworthy qualities, and purifying it with sublime, beneficial comportment by means of sound intellectual training. This is composed of three things: the first is increasing knowledge by means of study and God-consciousness (*taqwā*); the second is freeing oneself from the bonds of passions and caprice; and the third is purifying the soul by adorning it with the qualities of the Master. The noblest form of knowledge is knowledge of God and his Names and Qualities. The noblest form of freedom is a total escape from self-regard and self-satisfaction. The noblest form of self-purification is adopting every quality and attribute that is good, as defined by the intelligence and by the Law. Whoever attains these qualities achieves the highest rank and the loftiest station, and is adorned with the qualities of angelic perfection, and free of the attributes of animalistic imperfection. He has shed the oppressive darkness of his human attributes, and rid himself of the overwhelming power of caprice and natural avarice. Through this, he achieves a measure of nearness to the angels because of his intellectual and illuminated status, and he distances himself from the class of the lower animals. He attains a metaphorical link to the divine Qualities and shares in them—in a figurative sense, not in a perfect literal sense, because all created beings are flawed and the only perfect being is the One who has no peer in His Essence or His Qualities. Relative and figurative comparisons do not in any way imply essential equivalence, because having one thing in common does not mean having all things in common. Two opposites may have certain things in common even though they are as far apart as can be: black and white are opposites, but they are alike in that they are both accidents, colours and perceptible phenomena. An example is not identical with its object, nor is a comparison the same as an equivalence. The distinction between the Eternal and the created being is far greater than that between black and white.

❁ ❁ ❁

It is related that when ʿĀ'isha was asked about the character of the Prophet, may God bless him and give him peace, she replied, 'His character was the Qur'ān.' Likewise, God described him in His Book as being kind, merciful, just, a guide, generous, noble, relenting, forgiving, protecting, and forbearing; and He summed up all his noble characteristics by saying, *you are truly of an immense character.*[1]

The Prophet said, 'God has ninety-nine Names; the one who comprehends them all will enter Paradise.' Another narration has, 'the one who memorises them all will enter Paradise.' When it comes to comprehending the Names, there are three kinds of people: those who comprehend them with belief and faith through narration and transmission; those who comprehend them with memorisation, enumeration, understanding, action and state; and those who comprehend them with invocation, memorisation, knowledge, care, gnosis, emulation, unveiling, witnessing, glorification and magnification. The Lawgiver promised Paradise to all three of these groups,

1 Q.LXVIII.4.

but the Paradise of each will be commensurate with the height of their stations, the level of their states, the mastery of their gnosis, and the strength of their certitude. It will differ according to what was unveiled to them of the understanding of the secrets of the Names and Qualities, and the extent to which they emulated them and realised them, and to what degree they witnessed the manifestation of the qualities of the divine Essence. The 'collecting' encouraged in the text is ambiguous, and can be understood in a general or a specific sense. Consider the relevance of this to the Prophet's words, 'In Paradise there are one hundred levels, and the space between each two levels is like the space between heaven and earth. God has prepared them for those who struggle in His cause.'

The *ḥadīth* also shows that if a person gives one of the Names of God its proper due, he will attain one of these levels, and the one who comprehends them all will attain all the levels. The one who acknowledges their perfection and recites them has submitted to God,[1] and he will benefit from this. The one who recognises and comprehends them is a believer, and he will have more still. The one who knows their meanings and acts in accordance with them, and adorns himself with their qualities, is a gnostic, and he will be blessed with direct witnessing. As to the one who knows this Name [*Allāh*], he will be strengthened by what he beholds of its awe and majesty, and blessed by added nearness, grace and favour. The one to whom is revealed the secret of its wisdom will break free of his human shell, and the resplendent majesty of his Lord's might will shine forth for him, and he will realise the true meaning of pure humble servitude (*ʿubūdiyya*); for the reality of the divine Name is the divine Authority, and the nature of Godhood is might, grandeur, glory, exaltedness, and absolute power and self-sufficiency. God says, *Say, 'Who is Lord of the heavens and the earth?' Say, 'Allāh',*[2] *Say, 'Allāh', and then leave them.*[3]

It is the Greatest Name, for an authentic *ḥadīth* tells that the

1 Literally, 'is a *muslim*'.

2 Q.XIII.16.

3 Q.VI.91.

Prophet, may God bless him and give him peace, was asked about God's Greatest Name and answered, 'It is *Allāh*, the Living, the All-Sustaining (*Allāh al-Ḥayy al-Qayyūm*).' It is the Holy Name, blessed and transcendent; the Name of His Essence, described by His Qualities. It has precedence over all the other Names, and outstrips them in nobility and might. The other Names can be said to be Qualities, or the Qualities can be said to be Names, depending on one's point of view; but the quality of Godhood encompasses them all.

Know that God's Qualities (*ṣifāt*), as far as we are able to know and understand them, are of three kinds. Firstly, there are those that are known by revelation, and that may not be used or affirmed until permission has been given for them [to be so]. God Almighty may not be named by any name except that by which He named Himself, or for which He gave permission, or by which His Messenger, may God bless him and give him peace, named Him, and upon which his community agreed. He may not be named after any qualities that are not possible for him; for example, He may not be called 'understanding' (*ʿāqil*), 'perceptive' (*faqīh*), 'clever' (*labīb*), 'liberal' (*sakhiy*), or the like. Imam Mālik disliked that He be called in prayer, 'Oh my liege' (*yā sayyidī*), or 'Oh tender one' (*yā ḥannān*), or that He be called, 'friend' (*khalīl*), or 'beloved' (*ḥabīb*), or 'pure' (*ṣafī*), or 'beautiful' (*jamīl*), or 'pleasant' (*malīḥ*). He may not be referred to or described in absolute terms by things which He attributed to Himself in His Book in specific contexts, such as when He said, *He deceives them,*[1] *God plotted,*[2] *God scoffs at them,*[3] or *God sends astray,*[4] because these were said in the context of a response, recompense and requital for the actions of certain people and a mirroring back to them of their own attributes. Such things are descriptions of certain actions and requitals, but they

1 Q.IV.142.
2 Q.III.54.
3 Q.II.15.
4 Q.XIV.27.

are names from which God has absolved Himself, and His sublime Essence and holy Qualities are transcendently beyond being characterised by them.

Then there are those Qualities which are intrinsic to His Essence and by which He has been described for all eternity, and always will be, and it is impossible that this could ever not be so. They are such Qualities as the Living (*Ḥayy*), the Knowing (*ʿĀlim*), the Willing (*Murīd*), the Powerful (*Qādir*), the Hearing (*Samīʿ*), the Seeing (*Baṣīr*), the Speaking (*Mutakallim*), and the other essential Names from among the Most Beautiful Names.

Then there are those Qualities which are active. The Maker took these as Names because all actions come from Him. All temporal beings are connected with His speech and with His utterance 'Be!'. 'Be!' is the command for bringing into existence. The divine Power brings the action into existence and makes it come to pass and manifest; the divine Knowledge encompasses it, arranges it and reveals it; the divine Will directs it, designs it and perfects it; and the divine Hearing, Seeing and Speech are proof of the perfection of the One endowed with them. The power, will and knowledge of the temporal being do not affect the Eternal; nor do the Power and Will of God affect His own Essence or His eternal Qualities, they affect only the creating and shaping of temporal beings. The Real knows His Essence and His Qualities, and sees Himself, and hears His own Speech.

❁ ❁ ❁

The scholars have divided the meanings of the Most Beautiful Names into Four Categories. Firstly, those that refer to the blessed, holy, noble, mighty, eternal, transcendent Essence. They are those Names that refer to the existence of His Essence and refer to His Self, such as 'Thing' (*Shay'*), 'Being' (*Mawjūd*), 'Essence' (*Dhāt*), 'Deity' (*Ilāh*), 'Ancient' (*Qadīm*), 'Everlasting' (*Bāq*), 'Eternal' (*Dā'im*), 'Timeless' (*Azalī*), 'Self-Sustaining' (*Qayyūm*), 'One' (*Wāḥid*), 'Unique' (*Fard*),

'Singular' (*Witr*), 'Absolute' (*Ṣamad*), 'First' (*Awwal*), 'Last' (*Ākhir*), 'Outward' (*Ẓāhir*), 'Inward' (*Bāṭin*), 'Praised' (*Ḥamīd*), 'Real' (*Ḥaqq*). Any of these Names is the name of the Sublime Essence, and it can be said that it is [identical to] the Name and to the Named.

The second category of His Names are those that refer to a quality of the Eternal Essence; they are those that cannot be said to be It or other than It, nor that the name is the Named. They are those for which the name indicates a quality of His Essence. This category is itself divided into four types. There are those that are qualities of the Self of the Almighty Creator such as life (*ḥayā*), knowledge (*ʿilm*), power (*qudra*), will (*irāda*), hearing (*samaʿ*), sight (*baṣar*), and speech (*kalām*). Then there are those that pertain to His Will such as the Compassionate (*Raḥmān*), the Merciful (*Raḥīm*), the Forgiving (*Ghafūr*), the Clement (*ʿAfuw*), the Forbearing (*Ḥalīm*), the Loving (*Wadūd*), the Subtle (*Laṭīf*), the Patient (*Ṣabūr*), the Kind (*Karīm*), the Tender (*Ra'ūf*), the Generous (*Jawwād*), the Thankful (*Shakūr*). Then there are those that pertain to his Power such as the Strong (*Qawiyy*), the Overwhelming (*Ghālib*), the Conqueror (*Qāhir*), the Immovable (*Dhu'l-Quwwa al-Matīn*), the All-Powerful (*Qādir*), and other Names such as these.[1]

The third category of His Names are those that refer to the qualities of His Actions, and for these it can be said that they are other than It [the Essence], and that the name is not identical to the Named. They are those for which the name indicates a quality of one of His Actions, such as Maker (*Bāri'*), Shaper (*Muṣawwir*), Creator (*Khāliq*), Bestower (*Wahhāb*), Life-Giver (*Muḥyī*), Death-Bringer (*Mumīt*), Provider (*Rāziq*), the Expander (*Bāsiṭ*), the Grasper (*Qābiḍ*), the Exalter (*Rāfiʿ*), the Debaser (*Khāfiḍ*), the Honourer (*Muʿiz*), the Humbler (*Mudhil*), the Arbitrator (*Ḥakam*), the Just (*ʿAdl*), the Beautifier (*Muḥsin*), the Graceful (*Mufḍil*), the Opener (*Fātiḥ*), the Sender (*Bāʿith*), the Watcher

1 The author describes only three types. Given the context, one might speculate that the fourth he had in mind was the category of Names pertaining to the divine Knowledge such as the Knower (*ʿAlīm*), the Aware (*Khabīr*), the Counter (*Muḥṣī*), the Witness (*Shāhid*), and so on.

(*Raqīb*), the Inheritor (*Wārith*), the Answerer (*Mujīb*), the Sufficer (*Kāfi*), the Nourisher (*Muqīt*), the Healer (*Shāfi*), the Reviver (*Muʿāfi*), the Giver (*Muʿṭī*), the Withholder (*Mānīʿ*), the Reliable (*Wakīl*), the Vast (*Wāsiʿ*), the Equitable (*Muqsiṭ*), the Gatherer (*Jāmiʿ*), the Harmer (*Ḍār*), the Benefactor (*Nāfiʿ*), the Beginner (*Mubdi'*), the Returner (*Muʿīd*), the Guide (*Hādī*), the Infallible (*Rashīd*), the Promoter (*Muqaddim*), the Postponer (*Mu'akhkhir*), the Relenting (*Tawwāb*), the Good (*Bār*), the Avenger (*Muntaqim*), the Helper (*Muʿīn*), the Patron (*Walī*), the Clarifier (*Mubīn*), and other Names such as these.

The fourth category of His Names are those that refer to qualities of transcendence, and for these it can be said that they are identical to Him, and that the name and the Named are one, just like the Names of the Essence. They are the Names that negate all flaws from Him Exalted is He; such as the Almighty (*ʿAzīz*), the Compelling (*Jabbār*), the Proud (*Mutakabbir*), the Grand (*Kabīr*), the Master (*Mawlā*), the Sublime (*Mutaʿāl*), the Lord of Majesty and Bounty (*Dhu'l-Jalāl wa'l-Ikrām*), the Majestic (*Jalīl*), the Great (*ʿAẓīm*), the High (*ʿAliy*), the Protector (*Mu'min*), the Guardian (*Muhaymin*), the Rich (*Ghanī*), the Holy (*Quddūs*), Peace (*Salām*), and other Names such as these.

And then there is the Unique Name, glory be to it, which embodies all of these Names; all of them explain it, refer to it, and express it. The entire world,[1] from its heights to its depths, and all the wonders and mysteries within it, originate from this Name. [The world] is divided into two: the world of command (*ʿālam al-amr*) and the world of creation (*ʿālam al-khalq*). The world of command governs the world of creation, because it is closer to the Name of Godhood in the sublime order. Now when we say the Name of Godhood, we mean both this [Unique] Name and all the other Names, which are all equal with respect to their status as Names, but different with respect

1 By 'world' here, Ibn ʿAṭā' Allāh means the created order with all its levels; 'worlds' could be used here instead of 'world'.

to their implications. It is of this that God speaks when He says, *Say: Call upon Allāh, or call upon the Compassionate; whichever you call, He has the Most Beautiful Names.*[1] Though there are many Names, they all mean the same thing, which is *Allāh*, whom the Names describe; it is their origin and their source. The Names flow through the world even as spirits flow through bodies, and they have in it their locus just as the command has its locus in the creation; they adhere to it just as the accident adheres to the substance. Every being, be it immense or tiny, high or low, corporeal or ephemeral, common or rare, is surrounded by the Names of God both in essence and in nature. The Name of Godhood combines them all, just as the Names surround the worlds of command and creation and dwell in them as the spirit does in the body.

In His Kindness, through this Name God has divulged enough of His knowledge and power for the minds of His creatures to comprehend, so that they might be connected to Him. And in His grace, He has given them the natural ability (*fiṭra*) to know Him, and shown them the signs that point to Him. They testified to this and bore witness against themselves at the moment of *Am I not your Lord?*;[2] and even now He calls upon them to bear witness to this in their present existence by disclosing to them His Greatest Name, *Allāh*. It was for this that He taught it to them, and made it easy for them to pronounce, and made it ever present and accessible to them. He showed it to them plainly in the words *In the Name of Allāh, the Compassionate, the Merciful*, but due to its overwhelming obviousness it is not seen or recognised, and due to its constant affirmation it is forgotten and unacknowledged.[3] All things are put in order through it, and the most difficult things become easy through its invocation,

1 Q.xvii.110.

2 Allusion to Q.vii.172, *Remember when your Lord took the seeds of the sons of Adam from their loins and made them bear witness against themselves, and said, 'Am I not your Lord?' They replied, 'Indeed, we testify'—lest you should say on the Day of Resurrection, 'Of this we were unaware.'*

3 Ibn ʿAṭāʾ Allāh means that there is nothing that veils God but His omnipresence.

and it facilitates all needs and hopes. With it all efforts should be commenced. Neither heaven nor earth can contain it, nor can any throne or chair hold it; it is contained only by His Will, and in the hearts of those people for whom He destined goodness.[1] God places it by degrees into the hearts of those of His servants whom He chooses to honour with true servitude to Him, and He divulges its secrets to them. Glorious are His Names, and Majestic are His Qualities, and Magnificent is His Essence! A poet said,

> He is the Living, the All-Sustaining, glory be to Him;
> The mantle of might and grandeur is His robe.
> He enriched and nourished, and shone His light
> Upon all creation from earth to heaven.
> The earth is lit by the light of His beauty;
> His grace and guidance shower upon all.
> *Allāh, Allāh*, the Almighty strengthens us
> With the power to know the truth of *Allāh*.

۞ ۞ ۞

Know that all of the Qualities of God are the qualities and description of Godhood. One cannot say that they are He, nor that He is they, nor that they are something other than Him. This is because God is One and Self-Sustaining, and has no need for any other because of His Qualities. His Qualities are absolute and eternal, and sustained by Him, and they are infinite through the eternality and infinitude of His Essence. He is Necessary Being, and it is necessary that He be self-sufficient and it is impossible that He have need for any other thing. His Qualities have always existed and been known to Him, and it is not possible that He could exist without any of His Qualities, nor that His Qualities could exist without His Essence. Nor is it possible for anything to come between Him and them or that He would alter them in any way.

1 This is an allusion to the *ḥadīth*: Neither my Earth nor my Heavens can contain Me, but the heart of My believing servant can contain Me.

Yet, if He were they, then the Essence would be identical with the Qualities and the Qualities with the Essence, but it is impossible for a quality to indicate anything other than what it describes (*mawṣūf*), or for either of them to be separated from the other, because the quality is the form (*maʿnā*) and what it describes is the essence (*dhāt*), and it is impossible for a qualified thing to exist without that which qualifies it, and equally impossible for a quality to exist without what it describes.[1]

Furthermore, if the quality is [in every way] what it describes,[2] then this would mean that the quality would be identical with what it describes, which is impossible as we have just seen. It would also amount to affirming a quality while denying the essence, or removing the qualities from their essence, or separating one from the other; yet an essence must have qualities, and qualities must have an essence, because qualities cannot exist independently by their own essences, nor by their own beings, nor can they be independent of what they describe, just as the essence cannot be separated from its qualities. The one must exist alongside the other by logical and factual necessity, and they can no more be separated than a condition can be separated from that which it conditions. If one of them is negated or ceases to be, then so does the other. If one of them is affirmed or comes to be, then so does the other. One cannot imagine life except in a living thing, nor knowledge except in a knowing thing, nor will except in a willing thing. Likewise, neither power, hearing, sight, speech, or any other attribute can be imagined without the beings endowed with them.

On the other hand, if the Qualities were other than Him then they would either have to be extraneous to the Essence, or not. If

1 The argument here is that a quality is inseparable from what it describes, they have no existence without each other. Yet, a quality is limited to what it describes and cannot encompass the total reality of a thing. Applied to the Divine, the Qualities are *identified* with the Essence, they can describe It and It can be known through them. However, the Qualities are not *identical* to the Essence; the divine Essence contains the Qualities but they do not contain It as ultimately It is ineffable.

2 In the Arabic, this reads: 'if it were it' (*law kānat hiya huwa*).

extraneous, then they would either have to be self-sufficient, or reliant on something else. If they were self-sufficient, they would either have to be eternal or temporal. If the Quality were extraneous to the Essence, then It would be susceptible to change and It would be governed by what governs all other temporal beings, namely inevitable changes. If on the other hand the Qualities were not extraneous, then they would either have to be one with the Essence and identical with It, or distinct from It. It is impossible that they could be one with the Essence and identical with It because in that case they would be It; and if they were something other than the Essence, they would either have to be self-sufficient, or reliant on something else. It is impossible that they could be self-sufficient because this would amount to there being more than one distinct eternal being, which is contradictory to monotheism. Now, if they were also temporal realities, then they would have to be one of three things: either they would have been created in the Essence of the Eternal, or in something else, or in their own essence. If they were created in the Essence of the Eternal, this would mean that It was changed by their creation from other qualities which existed in It before, and that it is possible for It to change from qualities to others, and this [is impossible] since this indicates temporality, and is the nature of temporal bodies. And if these Qualities were created outside of It, then this would mean that what is describes by a quality could be qualified by a quality existing in something else but not in it, and if things could be qualified by qualities inherent outside of them, then everything would be the same, whether eternal or temporal, and it would be impossible for the world to contain things with different qualities because every single body would be alive, knowing, willing, powerful, and so on because it would share the qualities found in everything else. The logical conclusion of this would be that the qualities found in a temporal thing would be the same as the qualities found in the Eternal, and the qualities found in the Eternal would be the same as those found in temporal things, and they would share all the same laws [and this is impossible].

Therefore, it is impossible that God's Qualities could exist anywhere but in His Essence, because qualities cannot exist independently and cannot do without what they describe, for the mind cannot imagine a quality without a qualified object. And just as an eternal Quality must be beginningless, it must also endure forever without end, because it is impossible for an eternal Quality to change, and, in any case, He is above this because He is endowed with the Qualities of perfection, transcendence and majesty. His Qualities are not other than Him such that they could be separated from Him, nor are they identical with Him such that they could stand alone without being attributed to Him. They are not Him, nor are they other than Him.

The difference between the Qualities of the Eternal and the qualities of a temporal being is that the quality of a temporal being changes when its opposite arises; for example, motion ceases when stillness arises, and so on for all other qualities and their opposites. Yet it is not possible for the Eternal to cease, or for any of His Qualities to cease, nor is it possible for Him to change. He is transcendently beyond opposites and counterparts, and beyond all the qualities of temporal beings.

✡ ✡ ✡

As to the difference between Absolute Being and contingent being, contingent being is never free from accidental qualities such as motion and stillness, life and death, directions and boundaries, meetings and separations, changes and opposites. If something is never free from temporal things and did not precede them, then it must also be temporal, and all temporal things require a creator to create them who is not the same as them, nor resembles them. If this creator were the same as them, then what is necessary for them would be necessary for it too, and what is possible for them would be possible for it, and it too would require a creator, and so on *ad infinitum*. The Absolute Being is the One who is free from accidental limitative changes and who is characterised by eternal fixed attributes; and if this were not the case, then He would not be eternal. His Qualities are those of perfection, might, sufficiency and majesty such as befit Him alone and cannot be shared. He is the One who cannot be divided, compiled or composed; He is the Beginninglessly Ancient, the Endlessly Eternal, the Absolutely Sufficient who needs none but Himself. His existence does not depend on any other, and He does not require anyone else for His Essence, His Perfection, His Qualities, His Sufficiency or His Acts. It is known to the intellectuals by logical proofs, and to the scholars by transmitted revelation, that the Qualities of God are eternal, beginningless, transcendent, and sufficient through His eternal sublime Essence, which is characterised by Absolute Being, transcendent beyond the qualities of limitation and constraint, sanctified beyond the classes of modality, direction and dimension. He Alone is One, characterised by a Unity that is rationally impossible to divide. He cannot be contained in thought, nor comprehended by the mind, nor envisaged by the imagination. No other being can be imagined that matches His Essence or His Qualities of Self-Sufficiency, Perfection, Power, Might and Majesty. He is transcendently beyond any contingent temporal being. *Say: Allāh is One. Allāh, the Eternally Sufficient. He begets not, nor was He begotten. There is nothing equal to Him.*[1] A poet said,

> Blessed are You, who cannot be described!
> What power do my words have to speak of You?
> You are transcendent, and ever have been,
> So, who among us could describe You?
> If the seven seas were turned to ink,
> We would still run out of words to write.
> You are as You have exalted Yourself,
> And we humans can only say but a little.

Know that His Names and Qualities are not arranged in any particu-

1 Q.CXII.1-4.

lar order, nor do any have to appear first or last. They do not depend on any limit or chronology, nor may He be described in terms of linearity or sequence. His strength is the nature of His power, and His power is His eternality; His desire is His will; His sight is the breadth of His knowledge; His knowledge is the object of His sight; His speech is absolute, not sequential. He knows by His sight, and sees by His knowledge. His treasures are in His speech; His power is in His will. He creates with His hand when He pleases, and with His word when He pleases, and with His will when He pleases, and with the meanings of His Qualities as He pleases. He does not speak out of necessity, nor does He direct speech to Himself. What He wills comes to pass, and what He wills not does not. The beginnings and ends of things are for Him like one single thing. His Qualities are not Him, but nor are they other than Him. His word is His command, and His command is His speech, and His speech is light, guidance, healing, mercy, clarity, and Qur'ān. It is an eternal Quality of His. His command is not the same as His creation. His word is the truth. To Him belong all dominion, all command, and the creation of all created things. His command is His word, 'Be!', through which all things came into existence, and through which all temporal things came to be. They originated with Him, and came into existence from Him. *To God belongs the command, before and after*;[1] that is, His command existed before creation and after it. All things came into being through His speech, and His speech is His command, and it is an eternal essential Quality of His. All His Qualities are individually perfect, complete, unlimited, and beyond time and sequence; for sequence in qualities is an attribute of created things and a means of causality. God is like unto no other thing in all His Qualities. His Qualities are eternal through His eternality, and existent through His identity. They are not subject to direction such that they could be directed in one way and not another, or perceived by one quality and not another. His Essence is not one essence among many so that it could be present in

1 Q.xxx.4.

one place and not another. He does not need to create things in any particular order, nor does He think about things in the way temporal beings do such that He could be distracted by one thing from another. He is not affected by accidents causing him to react or move. He does not create with tools such that He would use the help of another. Nothing is too difficult for His power such that He would have to exert more effort to achieve it. His knowledge is such that He could never be ignorant of anything; His sufficiency is such that He could never be in need of anything; His power is such that He could never be incapable of anything; His strength is such that He could never be weak; His eternality is such that He could never cease to exist; His capability is such that He could never tire; His acts are such that He could never become disinterested; His capacity for creation is such that He could never become lethargic. His will has no beginning; His Qualities never change; His Essence never alters; His perfection is never impaired. Glory be to Him! A poet said,

> Glory be to Him whose qualities of perfection
> Are manifest in His perfection, beauty and majesty.
> He gives and withholds, and all desirable things
> Are subject to His will to give or deny.
> The servant is utterly veiled and powerless,
> And to God he ought to devote himself entirely,
> For he cannot help himself nor can anyone help him,
> With so short a life, and such scanty means.

When the Real speaks, He manifests; and when He wills, He ordains; and when He wishes, He reveals; and whatever He wills comes to pass. He is mighty despite His nearness, and near despite His transcendence. His Essence is veiled by His Qualities, and His Qualities are veiled by His actions. He unveils His knowledge by His will, and reveals His will by His power, and shows His power through motions. He conceals His design within His creations, and reveals it through causality. He is inwardly hidden in His unseen realm, but outwardly manifest in His wisdom. His power is disguised in His will, and His will is His wisdom, and His wisdom is manifested in His decree, which is the channel through which His power flows. His subtlety is hidden in His design, which is the manifestation of His will. He has no rival in His design, nor any equal in His craft.

[The Letters of the Unique Name]

Now this Unique Name of the Godhead is composed of four letters: *alif, lām, lām*, and *ḥā'*, as the poet said:

> Four letters in which my heart is absorbed,
> And into which my concerns and thoughts have disappeared:
> *Alif*, by which creation was assembled (*ta'allaf*) by design,
> *Lām*, to signify the way of self-reproach (*malāma*),
> Another *lām* to add to the meanings,
> Then a *hā'* through which I love (*uhīm*) and comprehend.[1]

Each of these letters has a special meaning, just as every one of God's Names has a special meaning. The *alif* comes from love (*ulfa*) and union (*ta'līf*); God united all of His creation in recognition of His Oneness and acknowledgement of Him as their God, Maker, Creator and Provider. God says, *If you ask them who created them, they will say, 'Allāh'*,[2] *If you ask them who created the heavens and the earth, they will say, 'Allāh'*.[3] *Allāh* was, and there was nothing with Him; and He is now as He ever was. There was nothing before Him, and there will be nothing after Him, as he said, 'I was a hidden treasure, and I wanted to be known, and so I created creation and made them know Me, and they knew Me.' And He united the hearts of His servants in love for Him and worship and obedience to Him in faith and *tawḥīd*, as He said, *Had you spent all that is in the world entire, you would not have been able to unite their hearts; but God united them, for He is Mighty, Wise*.[4] He also

1 These lines are attributed to the Persian saint Manṣūr al-Ḥallāj (d. 922).
2 Q.XLIII.87.
3 Q.XXXI.25.
4 Q.VIII.63.

united their voices in recognition of His worship and acknowledgment of His Oneness of Lordship. God says, *All in the heavens and the earth shall come to the Compassionate as a servant.*[1] A poet said,

> Blessed be Him whose servant I am proud to be,
> Glory be to Him, glory be to Him, and may He be praised.
> There is no dominion but His, mighty is He,
> He is the First in His authority, and the Last.

He united the hearts of His servants with grace, favour and blessing, and made it part of the provision He gave them; sometimes He withholds, and sometimes He gives forth. God says, *I created the jinn and man only that they might worship Me; I desire of them no provision, nor do I desire that they nourish Me.*[2]

✡ ✡ ✡

Alif is also the first letter of the Arabic alphabet, and the one that serves as a guide to the knowledge of its meanings, like a curtain that opens unto it and an image that represents it without being located in it. The meanings of words were not placed in the letters themselves, because their meanings are located elsewhere; the meanings of words are like their spirits, and the letters are like their bodies, and God made them into images and shells. The letters are the voices of a person's actions because they are actions manifested in their objects, and their meanings are knowledge manifested in its object.

Know that *alif* is the noblest, greatest and most important of all the letters. It is like the Adam of the letters, and the *hamza* that accompanies it[3] is like Eve; masculine words are like their male child, and feminine words like their female child. The other twenty-seven letters are born from the *alif*, just as all the progeny of Adam are from Adam. All the letters are from the *alif*, which is the root of them and

1 Q.XIX.93.
2 Q.LI.56–57.
3 The glottal stop that begins the letter *alif* when it is pronounced at the beginning of a word or phrase.

stands tall and straight.[1] The dot from which it is formed represents the basic principle of existence, which is the opposite of nothingness. The scholars of religious fundamentals (*ʿuṣūl al-dīn*) call this the singular substance (*al-jawhar al-fard*),[2] which is a way of expressing the affirmation of existence. Yet because it wished to be called by the name of *alif*, after being called by the quality of firstness, it extended by way of manifestation and appearance, and came down from above to below,[3] in order to acknowledge its own existence to itself. Thus, it became an *alif*, and was called this because of how all the other letters depended on its existence. It is related that the first thing God created was a single drop, and He looked upon it with His awesome presence until it melted and began to flow, and its flow was the *alif*. He then made it the opening letter of His Book, and the first of His letters, and it was the first of the letters because of how they all flowed from it and were manifested through it. The drop was an unknown treasure, and then it manifested and came down that it might reveal itself to them and that they might know it and attribute themselves to it. Likewise, Adam, upon whom be peace, was created to be the precursor to his progeny and the first of them, and they knew him and attributed themselves to him. The letters were secrets that God concealed and placed within Adam when He created him; He did not place them within any of the angels. The letters then flowed from the tongue of Adam in the form of the arts of language and diverse words, all having outward appearances and inner realities, boundaries and apexes. The outward appearance is their names and images; the inner reality is their meanings and secrets; the boundary is their details and rulings; and the apex is their direct witnessing and unveiling.[4] So every permutation of letters stems from the *alif*, and the

1 Referring to the shape of the letter: ا.

2 i.e. the atom, the smallest indivisible substance.

3 This is an allegory based on the way the *alif* is written, as a straight line from top to bottom.

4 Reference to the oft-quoted *ḥadīth*, 'Every verse of the Qur'ān has an outward appearance and an inward reality; and every letter has a boundary; and every boundary has an apex.'

letters partake in the mysteries of meaning according to the extent to which God breathes into them the spirit of profound speech, wondrous judgement and rarefied knowledge. The image of the *alif* is the secret by which Adam, upon whom be peace, was distinguished, and through it specifically the Real taught him the names of all things.

Know also that when knowledge of the secret of *alif* is revealed to a person and he gains its realisation, he has been given knowledge of the secret of the *tawḥīd* of Oneness (*waḥdāniyya*) and elevated to the station of knowledge of the secret of Absolute Unity (*aḥadiyya*). If knowledge of the secret of the *lām* that accompanies the *alif*[1] is revealed to a person and he gains its realisation, he has been granted knowledge of the secret of the Prophetic message. After Adam, no one gained, real and perfect knowledge of the secrets of all the letters except for our prophet Muḥammad, may God give blessings and peace to them both and to all the prophets and messengers who came between them. This is why he was vouchsafed all the letters of the alphabet and all the meanings, knowledge and rulings they contain, and therefore said, 'I have been gifted with succinct speech (*ūtītu jawāmiʿ al-kalim*).'

God sometimes chooses to honour one of His servants by revealing to them the meaning of the secret of a single letter, or two, or more, according to the portion that was destined for them, and they might then use this for anything they desire for their religion or worldly life, and things will react to them according to their mastery and the breadth and scope of their knowledge. This will be for them a special distinction and a gift from God to them. Every letter has its own wondrous secret, and to it is assigned special, effective and targeted knowledge that serves as a key to unlocking speech, and leads the one who knows it to his goal and reveals to him extraordinary things and gives him access to precious matters that are known to the wise ones, sages and scholars.

The *alif* corresponds to the number one, which is the first and

1 Together they form the definite article *al*.

source of all other numbers. This symbolises the pillar of *tawḥīd*, through which everything in existence subsists. Just as God is Necessary Being, the First Being before whom there was nothing and whose Unity precedes all other things, just so the *alif* came before the first number and all those that come after it, and there was nothing before it. The origin of the *alif* was a single solitary drop, which represents the central point of the axis of the circle of existence in the realm of the letters, and represents likewise the original locus of existence from which all of the world originated and through which subsists the circle of justice and equilibrium. It also represents the affirmation of existence—meaning the opposite of nothingness—which is known as the solitary substance (*jawhar fard*) that cannot be divided or enumerated. It is the locus of the propensity for being—like the primordial matter (*hayūlā*)—for the letters from which all physical beings are constituted, and by means of which it is possible to perceive intellectual concepts. It also represents the name of the oneness of *tawḥīd*, which must be known first-hand and not merely learned by rote like other creeds.

Because of all this, the human being, the scion of Adam, has himself the stature of the *alif* and stands tall and upright, a beautiful and ennobling stature which God Himself praised when He said, *We created man in the most beautiful stature.*[1] By this he was ennobled and honoured above most other creatures, as God said in His Book: *We ennobled the sons of Adam and carried them upon the sea, and provided them with goodly things, and greatly honoured them above many of those We created;*[2] *Those who have faith and do righteous deeds; they are the best of creation.*[3] He is among the noblest of creatures, the best of beings, the most honoured of creations. One aspect of his preferment and ennoblement is that God made him a meeting-point of two seas,[4] the

1 Q.xcv.4.

2 Q.xvii.70.

3 Q.xcviii.7.

4 'The meeting-point of two seas' appears in the Qur'ān, Q. lv.19-20: *He has let loose the two seas; they come together; but an isthmus is between them, and they encroach not beyond it.*

lower sea of the darkness of animal desires, and the higher sea of the light of luminous intelligence, and placed him in two worlds, the world of the spiritual and the world of the corporeal, and in a single unit of prayer (*rakʿa*) He combined for him all the worship of the Supreme Assembly of angels who dwell in the seven heavens, with seven forms of worship; and He made the rewards of their worship return to the human being, with manifold increase. Some of them are ever standing in worship, others ever bowing down, others ever in prostration,[1] others ever praising. They worship God always without cease, and were created as pure, innocent lofty beings of spirit, light without darkness, intelligence without desire, subtlety without density, constancy without cease, vigour without languor, obedience without defiance, worship without reward, devotion without recompense, service without condition, union without separation. The human being, on the other hand, was made an isthmus, an intermediary creature standing between the worlds of light and darkness; and whichever of them is dominant in him is the one that defines him. Glory be to Him who brought these two opposites together and combined the attributes of both realms in this noble Adamic being, and made the locus of His intellect, knowledge, *tawḥīd*, love and secrets his untarnished heart. He is the straight path, the upright isthmus; by the *alif* He assembled him, gathered him, united him, distinguished him, separated him, and divided him. He composed (*allafa*) His Book from a drop, and created His creation from a drop, and He causes them to die with a grasp, and gives them life with a breath. A poet said,

> The *alif* has virtue and ascendance over
> The other letters, so seek no substitute.
> The most secret of knowledge is found within it;
> Truly unique in its majesty, and unbending;
> Eternally upright, one in number,
> Its form encompasses the sum and the parts.

1 This is a reference to the movements of the canonical prayer.

Letter and meaning brought together in secret;
Root and branch connected and joined.
Discover its secrets, if you have ambition;
Take its subtleties to heart, and ascend.
It is like a man whose nature embodies
Sublime knowledge, spirit, body and character,
An angel's intellect, an animal's instinct;
How glorious to know it, how dreadful to know not!

۞ ۞ ۞

The first *lām* [in the Name *Allāh*] is the possessive *lām*.[1] If the *alif* were omitted from the start of the Name, it would spell *lillāh* (to God), and God says: *To God* (lillāh) *belongs all that is in the heavens and all that is in the earth; and whether you reveal what is in your souls or hide it, Allāh shall reckon you for it;*[2] *Say, 'To whom belongs all that is in the heavens and the earth?' Say, 'To God* (lillāh), *who has ordained mercy upon Himself';*[3] *Say, 'To whom belongs the earth and everyone in it, if you know?' They will say, 'To God* (lillāh).*' Say, 'Then will you not reflect?' Say, 'Who is the Lord of the heavens and the Lord of the Mighty Throne?' They will say, 'To God* (lillāh)*';*[4] *If you disbelieve, then to God* (lillāh) *belongs all that is in the heavens and all that is in the earth; and God is Independent, All-Praised;*[5] *Truly, to God* (lillāh) *belongs all that is in the heavens and the earth. Truly, the promise of Allāh is real;*[6] *To God* (lillāh) *belongs the command, before and after.*[7] These verses and others like them all indicate and demonstrate the possessive *lām*. The *lām* also represents the tablet of the intellect (*lawḥ al-ʿaql*) and understanding for those whose breasts God expands and whose hearts and secrets he singles out, illuminating

1 The Arabic preposition *li* or *la*, written with a single letter *lām*, means 'of' or 'to' in the sense of 'belonging to'.

2 Q.II.284.

3 Q.VI.12.

4 Q.XXIII.84-87.

5 Q.XXVI.31.

6 Q.X.55.

7 Q.XXX.4.

their knowledge with the light of certitude and realisation, that they might behold Him. It also represents the tablet of prophethood and messengership (*lawḥ al-nubuwwa wa'l-risāla*) because it broadens and expands the breast and illuminates it with knowledge of the secrets, wisdoms and decrees of revelation.

The second *lām* represents the possessive *lām* again; for if the *alif* and the first *lām* are removed, what is left is *lah* ('to Him' or 'to Whom'). God says, *That is Allāh, your Lord; to Him belongs all dominion, and there is no god but He; so where, then, will you turn?*;[1] *Hollowed is He to Whom belongs the dominion of the heavens and earth and all that is between them, and Who has knowledge of the Hour*;[2] *Know you not that it is Allāh to Whom belongs the dominion of the heavens and the earth, to punish whom He will and forgive whom He will? Allāh is able to do all things*;[3] *He it is to Whom belongs the dominion of the heavens and the earth; there is no god but He, who gives life and deals death*;[4] *Allāh! To Him belongs the dominion of the heavens and the earth*;[5] *To Him longs the dominion of the heavens and the earth, and then to Him you shall return*;[6] *His Word is Truth, and to Him belongs the dominion.*[7] These verses and others like them indicate and demonstrate the possessive *lām*. He is the Sovereign and the Owner, and to Him belongs dominion of the heavens and the earth and all that is between them and all the realms they contain, from the highest to the lowest. A poet said,

> The secret of the *alif* flows in the *lām* just the same,
> So seek it out and do not stop at outward appearances.
> The secret of knowledge is found in the two *lām*s combined,
> Like the sun rising through the dawn at the end of the night.
> The *lām* tells that creation lies to one side

1 Q.XXXIX.6.
2 Q.XLIII.85.
3 Q.V.40.
4 Q.VII.158.
5 Q.IX.116.
6 Q.XXXIX.44.
7 Q.VI.73.

Of the *alif*, beyond any doubt or denial.
Seek out the wisdoms that lie within the *lām*,
And understand its meanings, if you have the mind for it;
You will find the realities of what was concealed before:
A mighty treasure, hidden from all other men.

❁ ❁ ❁

The letter *hā'* represents the absolute being of the Real, and an affirmation of His Oneness and His encompassment of all things in knowledge, will, power, possession and dominion. It is the *hā'* of the awe of splendour (*haybat al-bahā'*), and the glory of the divine. If the *alif* and the two *lāms* are removed, then all that remains is the letter *hā'*, which stands for *hū* ('He' or 'Him'). God says, *He is my Lord, there is no god but He. Upon Him have I placed my trust, and to Him I repent;*[1] *He is but One God;*[2] *Say, 'He, Allāh, is One';*[3] *He is the First and the Last, the Outwardly Manifest and the Inwardly Hidden; He has knowledge of all things;*[4] *He is Allāh, besides whom there is no god, the Knower of the unseen and the visible; He is the Compassionate, the Merciful;*[5] *He is Allāh, besides whom there is no god, the Sovereign, the Holy;*[6] *He is Allāh, the Creator, the Maker, the Shaper.*[7] These verses and others like them indicate and demonstrate the *hā'* of exceptionality and the uniqueness of the divine. The people concerned with literal meanings would say that a pronoun is defined by the words that precede and follow it because it needs an antecedent, so that the context of the speech is what gives it meaning. However, the people concerned with inner realities say that the pronoun does not need to be given meaning through context because it is the foremost of all known things and knowledge of it resides in the heart, where it is known as it truly is, along with its qualities. So,

1 Q.xiii.30.
2 Q.vi.19.
3 Q.cxii.1.
4 Q.lvii.3.
5 Q.lix.22.
6 Q.lix.23.
7 Q.lix.24.

if *hū* is uttered to them, the first thing they will think of is the Real, and they will require no further explanation. This is because of the depth of their gnosis, the breadth of their knowledge, the strength of their understanding, the perfection of their mastery of the realities of the divine nearness, the unique purity of their hearts, the dominance of the remembrance of the Real in their innermost secrets, and their immersion in the invocation of the Unique Name.

When one says *hū*, which is comprised of the letters *hā'* and *wāw*, the letter *hā'* originates in the back of the throat, and then the letter *wāw* originates from the lips; that is, they come from the beginning point and the end point of the area where the letters are vocalised. This symbolises an affirmation of the existence of known being, which is the opposite of nothingness, and also symbolises how every contingent being originates from Him and returns to Him, while He has no beginning. The letter *hā'* is one of the letters pronounced in the throat without the involvement of the tongue or the lips.

The *hā'* is also the first and last of the Most Beautiful Names, and the one that brings their total to one hundred, because it is contained within the Name *Allāh*, and it is with the *hā'* that the invocation of *Allāh* is completed. So, the Name begins with *alif* and ends with *hā'*, which completes it and perfects its meaning. Supplication and invocation begin with it, and it is the first and the last of the Most Beautiful Names. The first is 'O *Allāh*' and the last is 'O *Hū*'. This Name is the first and the last, the beginning and the conclusion.

The Almighty mentions this Name in many verses in His Book, such as, *He is the Living; there is no god but He;*[1] *He is the First and the Last, the Outwardly Manifest and the Inwardly Hidden;*[2] *He is Allāh, there is no god but He; to Him belongs all praise at the first and the last;*[3] *He is Allāh, besides whom there is no god, the Knower of the unseen and the visible; He is*

1 Q.XL.65.
2 Q.LVII.3.
3 Q.XXVIII.70.

the Compassionate, the Merciful;[1] *He is Allāh, besides whom there is no god, the Sovereign, the Holy;*[2] *He is Allāh, the Creator, the Maker, the Shaper; His are the Most Beautiful Names. All in the heavens and earth hymn His glory, and He is the Almighty, the Wise.*[3]

He is first, He is last,
He is Hidden and Manifest,
He is One, He is Owner,
He is Power, He is Knower,
He is Creator, He is Provider,
He is Just, He is Commander,
He is Judge, He is Informer,
He is Truth, He is Invoker,
He is Generous, He is Giving,
He is Merciful, Forgiving.

It is related that one of the great gnostics would supplicate only with this one Name, and ask God by it alone; he would say, '*Hū*, *Hū*, O You who none can know but You! I ask of You…', and he would name his request.

It is also related that Abū al-Qāsim al-Junayd, may God have mercy on him, said to one of his closest companions, 'The Supreme Name of God is *Hū*, because God first manifested it in His Name *Allāh*, and hid it in the end of the *hā'* in this Name. It is *Hū*, and it was so clearly manifest that eventually it became hidden and concealed until it was unknown, and was so widely invoked that eventually it became forgotten and left unmentioned.'[4]

One of those who had deep knowledge of the Unique Name said that if someone invokes the Name *Allāh* but does not pronounce

1 Q.LIX.22.
2 Q.LIX.23.
3 Q.LIX.24.
4 Ibn ʿAṭā' Allāh is referring to his earlier argument that God is only veiled by His omnipresence.

the *hā'* at the end properly as it ought to be, then he has not really invoked the Name at all. He made the proper pronunciation of the letter *hā'* a necessary requirement of the invocation of *Allāh*, whether in a state of invocation (*fī ḥāl dhikr*), or when saying the *takbīr* in the formal prayer or the call to prayer, or when reciting the Qur'ān.

One of the esteemed masters of both the Law and the spiritual Path used to say to his companions, 'If any one of you suffers a difficulty or a calamity, he should say, "*Allāh*, the Living, the All-Sustaining", for it is the Supreme Name.'

۞ ۞ ۞

It is related that the folk of *tawḥīd* are divided into four categories according to how they refer to *tawḥīd* in their invocations. The first group are those who say, 'There is no god but *Allāh*', which is a balance of negation and affirmation: a negation of doubts and misunderstandings, and an affirmation of the One beyond any partners or opposites.

The second group are those who say, '*Allāh*', invoking only the Unique Name without any negation but only a repeated affirmation; they deem that affirming and negating is desolate and distant [from the Name itself].

The third group are those who say, '*Hū, Hū*', which is the purest affirmation, the constant invocation which is light on the tongue; the invocation of the heart.

The fourth group are those who are silent and say nothing at all, and are absorbed in Him and oblivious to their own selves, lost in their witnessing of the One so that they need not invoke His Oneness. Their invocation is an act of witnessing, not a deed of the tongue.

۞ ۞ ۞

It is also said that those who have gnosis of this Name are of four kinds: one gnostic says, '*Allāh*', another says 'He (*Hū*)', another says,

'I (*Anā*)',[1] and another says nothing. A poet said,

> Existence is a matter of Law and gnosis,
> And there is much perplexity in seeking it.
> God is our Maker and all we will ever find,
> And the servant is in dire need of seeking Him.
> To invoke something other than Him is yet to invoke Him,
> For God is the most manifest being, and all exist through Him;
> All that a man can ever do for himself
> Is go on comparing and finding analogies.
> But how to get to the Invoked as you invoke Him?
> Everyone has their own path, which they follow.
> Silence is invocation of Him, so invoke this way and that,
> It is all invocation for Him, for invocation is analogy.

۞ ۞ ۞

Abū ʿĪsā al-Tirmidhī narrated on the authority of Anas b. Mālik that the Messenger of God, may God bless him and give him peace, said, 'The leader of all the verses in the Qur'ān (*sayyidat āy al-Qur'ān*) is the *Āyat al-Kursī*.'[2] The wisdom of it being the leader of all the verses of the Qur'ān, when it is only a single verse from it, is found in four things. The first is that it is unique in how it describes the Glorious Essence of God, and how it contains several Qualities of His and many instances of the pronoun that refers to His Essence, and how it presents the reality of *tawḥīd*. Note how every pronoun *hū* in the verse refers to God and not to other things, such as is the case for other verses that describe stories, parables, proclamations,

1 The gnostic who invoked *Anā* would be invoking the Divine 'I', quoting God's reference to Himself in the first person in the Qur'ān and elsewhere, as in, *There is no god but I, so worship Me* (Q. XXI.25)

2 *Allāh! There is no god but He, the Living, the All-sustaining. Slumber seizes Him not, neither sleep. To Him belongs all that is in the heavens and the earth. Who is there that shall intercede with Him, save by His leave? He knows what lies before them and what is after them, and they comprehend not anything of His knowledge save such as He wills. His Footstool covers the heavens and earth, and the preserving of them oppresses Him not; He is the Sublime, the Glorious.* (Q.II.255)

promises, warnings, descriptions, encouragements, prohibitions and commandments. This means that every verse in the Qur'ān is subservient to this one, because everything other than the divine Essence is subservient to It, and all the things they [the other verses] describe about God's essential Qualities are summed up in this one verse in eleven pronouns, as well as the five proper Names. There is nothing greater than the mention of the divine Essence, because It comprises all the Qualities and is therefore the greatest thing that can be mentioned, the most precious treasure and the most valuable gift.

Secondly, the verse is distinguished by how often the Name of the Essence is concealed within it by the pronoun referring to It in the form of the letter *hā'*, which encompasses the foundations of the Names of the Essence and the perfection of the Qualities. The *hā'* contains a wondrous mystery and many marvellous secrets, and it has been said that if someone continues to invoke *Hū*, he will be bathed in its lights and shown its secrets.

Thirdly, it was given the name *Āyat al-Kursī* (the Verse of the Footstool) and became known by it; the Footstool covers the heavens and the earth and more besides, although they are all His creations. This shows how different His creations can be in magnitude and displays His limitless power, although He extends His grace and mercy to whomsoever of His creatures He will. Likewise, He favoured the *Āyat al-Kursī* above all the other verses in the Qur'ān and graced it with the Name of His Essence, even though all of the Qur'ān is His Speech and all of His Qualities, and all His Names are contained within it. Thus He singles out for distinction whichever of His Words and Names He will.

Fourthly, the Prophet, may God bless him and give him peace, called it a 'leader' and chose this particular title for it and it alone among verses. The word 'leader' is as expression of the utmost praise, distinction and favour. Consider how he said, 'I am the leader of the sons of Adam.' He then showed the virtue of his humility and the perfection of his leadership and nobility by expressing gratitude to God for His favour by adding, 'and I say this without pride (*wa-lā fakhr*)'. This merited him the utmost degree and favour; for the nobility of a name lies in the nobility of the named, and the nobility of knowledge lies in the nobility of the subject, as a poet said,

> God is most Great without comparison or analogy;
> He is the Great, and that is His rightful description.
> He added a Name to show you His manifestation –
> Look around at creation, and then look at how He humbles it.

Know also that the pronoun *hū* can refer to all living beings whether intelligent or not and whether they have language or not, as well as to all inanimate objects such as stones, trees, plants, gases, and all other things.[1] This symbolises how the invocation [of God] is carried out by all, whether the human being with his tongue and the motions of his body, or the constant invocation of the heart as it beats over and over without ever pausing, or the breaths of the sleeping person as he sleeps, or the sick person as he moans in pain, or the lion as it roars, or the wolf as it howls, or the horse as it whinnies, or the donkey as it brays, or the wind as it blows, or the bird as it sings, or the plants as they sway and move, or the inanimate object as it sits still, or the water as it ripples and flows. They all hymn the glory of their Creator and proclaim His existence with the pronoun *hā'*, according to their situations, which all symbolise '*Hū, Hū*'. God says, *The heavens and the earth and all they contain hymn His glory, and there is not a thing that does not hymn His praises, though you understand not their hymns. He is ever Forbearing, Forgiving.*[2] To glorify God means to declare His transcendence, and this is the innate invocation [in all things] of which all that can be understood is that these things affirm the existence of the Existentiator of all things, the All-Powerful One who is transcendently free of the attributes of contingent beings—glory be to Him!

1 There is no neuter gender in Arabic, so the pronoun *hū* can mean either 'he' and 'it', and *hā* either 'she' or 'it', depending on the word.

2 Q.xvii.44.

A poet said,

> Majestic is the Almighty! Everything in existence
> Invokes Him with countless expressions and languages.
> Everything has its own way of invoking:
> The animal, the plants, even the lifeless objects.
> Each has a language, each hymns His glory,
> Each declares His transcendence above all else.
> He it is whose knowledge encompasses them all,
> While their thoughts cannot possibly encompass Him.

It is related that Abū Bakr al-Shiblī, may God have mercy on him, said, 'I came across a lively young Ethiopian girl who was running and racing about. I said to her, "O maidservant of God, calm down and be easy on yourself." She replied, "*Hū, hū.*" I said to her, "Where did you come from?" She replied, "*Hū.*" I said, "Where are you going?" She replied, "*Hū.*" I said, "What do you want from *hū*?" She replied, "*Hū.*" I said, "What is your name?" She said, "*Hū.*" I said, "How many times have you said *hū* now?" She replied, "I will keep on saying *hū* until I meet *hū*." Then she said,

> '"Ah my beloved ones, I have no replacement for you,
> '"And I have nothing else to seek but you.
> '"Because of my madness for you, they called me sick,
> '"And I answered, 'I hope I am never cured!'"'

Shiblī continued, 'So I said to her, "Maidservant of God, what do you mean by *hū*? Do you mean God?" But when she heard the Name of God, she took an enormous gasp and fell down dead, may God have mercy on her! I wanted to take her away to be prepared for burial, but a voice called out, "Shiblī! If someone goes mad out of love for Us, and seeks Us with ardour and invokes Us with passion, and dies by Our Name, then leave them for Us, for We shall pay their ransom." I looked to see who was calling, and she had disappeared when I looked back. I do not know if she was raised up or buried. May God have mercy on her.'

A poet said,

> What is love, other than to die in passion,
> Turning a deaf ear to all besides that in which you
> are annihilated?
> She tells them all kinds of things with her words,
> But they are already infatuated by her beauty.

۞ ۞ ۞

Consider, then—may God grant you success—this Unique Name and how it embodies all these meanings in its individual letters and their combination. It is the Supreme Name, the Name of Godhood by which all created beings were ordained, and by which the earth was spread out and the heavens lifted. The splendour of Paradise was made for those who invoke it, and the flames of Hell were stoked for those who deny it. The kings of this earth have only worldly dominion, not true sovereignty; they inherit and pass on their kingship until their line is broken or their kingdom toppled. This Unique Name is the Name of the Essence, and in it are combined dominion, sovereignty and the *hā'* that encompasses all. Is this not what absolute sovereignty must be? God says, *Allāh is the light of the heavens and the earth*;[1] that is, their Creator, Maker and Illuminator, before which they did not exist. And He says, *We shall inherit the earth and all who are upon it, and to Us they shall return*;[2] *Know you not that it is Allāh to whom belongs the dominion of the heavens and the earth, to punish whom He will and forgive whom He will? Allāh is able to do all things.*[3]

Each individual part of this Unique Name contains its own wondrous secrets, meanings and wisdoms, and marvels of knowledge and gnosis; and in the complete Name, *Allāh*, are others more wondrous and marvellous still. Seek them out and understand them, and you will find them, God willing.

1 Q.XXIV.35.
2 Q.XIX.40.
3 Q.V.40.

O striving seeker of the secret of the Names,
Seek, and you shall be guided to your noble aim.
Search for it and you shall find, in its letters,
A wondrous meaning from the clearest traditions.
Perfection rises in it to the highest horizons,
Far above the reaches of any deception.
A glorious root extends through all gnosis,
So, hear its meanings by the mouth and the ear.
It is the faith whose substance is in *tawḥīd*,
By a Mighty Name that awaits the sagacious gnostic.
He is the Precious One who gave all existence value,
From the heights to the depths, nothing would be without Him.
The secret of *alif* flows to the *hā'* concealed there,
The understanding of which is the greatest of gifts.
The letter at its start is the might of its substance;
The letter at its end is a spirit without body.
Its letters are four, so seek out their meanings,
And you shall be graced by its wisdom at all times.
It is the *alif* followed by the two *lāms*,
And then the ever-decisive *hā'*.
Allāh, the Unique Name of the Essence!
Know its reality, O trusted one!
Invoke it always, if you have any aspiration,
And know its proper decorum to save you from harm.
By it you may raise veils and, by it, cure many ills;
By it you may alleviate anguish from those who suffer;
By it you may extract a pearl from the ocean of gnosis;
By it you may rise up through the stations towards home.
Strive for it with your all at every opportunity;
Preserve its secrets from any who might be misguided.
Those who do not attain this have scanty prospects
In this life and the next, and may well be deceived.
Those who understand it will be illuminated,
Like the dawn that is lit up by verses and traditions.
Pearls are not too dear for those who seek them,
Even if the highest price is charged;

The pearl of beauty will not simply float up to you;
You must plunge the depths to claim it for yourself.
May you ever remain in the care of your Lord,
As long as winds blow, waves roll, and ships sail.

God willing, we will relate the rest that we have understood with our minds, or heard and been taught by our masters, may God have mercy on them and be well pleased with them, in the second part of this book about the knowledge of this Unique Name and its meanings. Let the seeker reflect on this and number it among the most precious knowledge he can attain, for it contains many subtle and beautiful meanings, teachings, secrets and wisdoms, by which he will greatly benefit, God willing. Anyone given the grace to have its doors opened for him should look, and he will find; and understand, and he will benefit, by the grace of God.

Here ends the first part of the book, praise be to God for all His favours. May God bless our master Muḥammad, the Seal of His Prophets. It will be followed, God willing, by the second part, which is concerned with the benefits and wisdoms of the Name. May God help us with it, for there can be no strength save through Him.

PART TWO

On the Knowledge of the Perfection and Nobility of the Name *Allāh*, and an Explanation of Its Mysteries and the Unique Benefits of Invoking It, by God's Power

God says, *O you who have faith, invoke Allāh abundantly, and hymn His glory in the morn and the eve;*[1] *Those who invoke Allāh standing, seated, and on their sides.*[2] The Messenger of God, may God bless him and grant him peace, said, 'The unique ones (*mufradūn*) will be foremost.' They asked, 'Who are the unique ones, O Messenger of God?' He answered, 'Those who invoke God often, be they men or women.' He also told us that God says, 'If someone invokes Me so much that He has no time to ask of Me, I will give him more than I give those who ask.' He also said, 'The most difficult deeds are three: honesty with oneself, helping one's brother financially, and remembrance of God Almighty.' He also said, 'A person can perform no action more likely to save him from God's punishment than the remembrance of God.' Al-Ḥasan asked the Messenger of God about the best of actions, and he replied, 'That you should die and your tongue be moist with the remembrance of God.'

See, then, may God give you success, how this Name—*Allāh*, the Name of God—is the best of all acts of worship. This is because God has appointed specific times and amounts for all other acts, but has not prescribed any specific time or amount for this Name, but has simply encouraged us to invoke it often, saying, *Invoke Allāh abundantly;*[3] *The*

1 Q.XXXIII.41–42.
2 Q.III.191.
3 Q.XXXIII.41.

men who invoke Allāh oft and the women you invoke Allāh oft—for them Allāh has prepared forgiveness and a glorious reward;[1] *Invoke Allāh oft, that you might succeed;*[2] *Invoke Allāh as you invoke your forefathers, or with an even more vigorous invocation.*[3]

The Messenger of God, may God bless him and grant him peace, said, 'Those who invoke *Allāh* often, be they men or women, are the foremost and the triumphant.' It is related that in the Torah is written, 'The Irresistible One rose, in His glory, above all glories, and the waters raged and clashed in awe of Him. Then the Almighty Majestic One called out: "I am God; there is no god but I. Whoso invokes Me, I invoke him; whoso asks Me, I give unto him."'

It is also written there, 'He said, "Moses! I am God, the Eternal, the Timeless, the Creator of Mecca; I impoverish the adulterers, and abandon those who abandon prayer; I raise prices when demands are high, and lower them when demands are low. Such is God, your Lord, so worship Him."'

We have spoken about this Name in the light of what has been taught about it, and the understanding God has inspired of it. Now you should know that the point of all this is to encourage this Name to be invoked, and invoked more often than anything else, because of the love God has for it, and its tremendous standing in His sight, and the special virtue and nobility He has assigned to its invocation above all other invocations. The purpose of this is to provoke meditation on its mysteries, so that its resplendent lights are shone upon the heart and the body, and so that the gnosis and love of the one who invokes it is strengthened, and he is drawn ever closer to God. The sign of love is the frequent invocation of the Beloved; the sign of increase is the frequent offering of thanks to Him; the sign of grace is obedience to His commands and prohibitions; and the sign of contentment is

1 Q.XXXIII.35.
2 Q.VIII.45.
3 Q.II.200.

the offering of worship to Him during moments of leisure, and the preference of good over evil. A poet said about this,

> Repeat to me the mention of His Names,
> And polish hearts with His light and brilliance,
> And fill the glasses for the souls,
> For they are yearning to drink.
> A Name from which the universe took its light,
> On earth, sea and sky;
> The minds of men are dazzled by its qualities,
> The hearts of men are brightened by its light.
> When its majesty is revealed to hearts,
> They sense the mystery of its glory and brilliance.
> The hearts of the righteous are glad to be near it;
> It takes them up to its highest heights.
> The repetition of His Name
> Is the dearest of His blessings to the gnostics.

❁ ❁ ❁

One of the special qualities of this Unique Name is to be found in every word of *Sūrat al-Ikhlāṣ* [Q.cxii] which has its own special allusion and wondrous meaning, and which imparts mystery, knowledge, and spiritual insight. Observe: *Say* alludes to a command, *He* to an affirmation of His Being, *Allāh* to the Name of God, *One* (*Aḥad*) to His Unique Oneness, *Allāh* to the invocation of the Unique Name of divine Oneness, *the Self-Sufficient* (*Ṣamad*) to the Essence's transcendence beyond the human soul, *He begets not* to His perfect transcendence beyond all other than Him, *nor is He begotten* to His eternality, timelessness and beginninglessness, and *none is like Him* to the absence of any opposite, counterpart, comparison or rival to Him.

This Name is called the 'Unique Name' because of how it is repeated and how it stands alone between the final Name ['He,' *Hū*] and the name 'the Self-Sufficient' (*Ṣamad*); the Almighty Real chose this Name and made it unique, and repeated it so that it would be repeated by others. He also chose it as the Name for the divine Essence; by means of this Name, the Essence was revealed and given mention and renown in existence. He says: *Say: Allāh, then leave them to their idle talk,*[1] and: *He is Allāh in the heavens and earth*;[2] that is, He is worshipped, invoked, praised and thanked, and all creatures are under His command and prohibition. He knows the treachery of the eye and what the heart conceals,[3] and nothing in the universe is beyond His ken.

Likewise, regarding the phrase 'God most Great' (*Allāhu Akbar*), there are five perspectives. Firstly, it means that God's remembrance of Himself and His Oneness, Magnificence and Glory is greater and mightier than the remembrance of His poor weak creatures and their declaration of His Oneness; for He is Independent, All-Praised.

Secondly, the invocation of this Name is greater than the invocation of any of the other Names.

Thirdly, God's remembrance of His servant in pre-eternity, before he came into existence, is greater, mightier, and earlier, older, more complete, more brilliant, loftier, nobler and kinder than the servant's remembrance of God now. God says, *The remembrance of Allāh is greater*.[4]

Fourthly, the remembrance of *Allāh* in prayer is better and greater than the remembrance of Him outside of prayer; and to witness the Object of remembrance in the prayer is mightier, greater and more perfect than prayer itself.

Fifthly, God's remembrance of you with these manifold blessings and boons, and the favour He does you by calling you to obey Him, is greater than your remembrance of Him in acknowledging them, since you cannot thank Him as He should be thanked. Therefore,

1 Q.VI.91.
2 Q.VI.3.
3 Allusion to Q.XL.19.
4 Q.XXIX.45.

our Prophet, may God bless him and grant him peace, said, 'I cannot praise You; You are as You have praised Yourself.' Though he was unsurpassed in his knowledge, status and gnosis, he confessed his inability to praise God.

Moreover, after the affirmation of God's Oneness there is nothing greater than prayer (*ṣalāt*), which is why it is the second Pillar of Islam; according to the words of the Prophet, may God bless him and grant him peace, 'Islam is built on five: Declaring God's Oneness, prayer...,' and so on. The start of the prayer is heralded by the words *Allāhu Akbar*, and only this divine Name will do, and no other; the Prophet, may God bless him and grant him peace, said, 'It is consecrated by the *takbīr*.'[1] This Name is also mentioned in the call to prayer, and in every *takbīr* of the prayer.

۞ ۞ ۞

The invocation of this Name, then, is better than any other form of worship, and is closer to intimate discourse (*munājāt*) than prayer or any other form of worship. A *ḥadīth* tells us that God Almighty says, 'I am the companion of the one who remembers Me.' He also says, 'I am as My servant thinks of Me, and I am with him when he remembers Me. When he remembers Me to himself, I remember him to Myself. When he remembers Me alone, I remember him alone. When he remembers Me in a group, I remember him in a better group.'[2] God says, *Remember Me; I will remember you.*[3]

The proof that invocation [of the Name *Allāh*] is better than prayer is found in the same aforementioned verse. God says, *Prayer preserves from iniquity and abomination...*,[4] which indeed it does, and it is a tremendous thing; but the remembrance of *Allāh* is greater than

1 The *takbīr* is to say *Allāhu Akbar*. The *takbīr* starts the call to prayer, is pronounced at the beginning of the canonical prayers and also initiates the different movements of the canonical prayer.

2 Narrated by Muslim.

3 Q.II.152.

4 Q.XXIX.45.

it, and greater than every other form of worship, for God then says, *...yet the remembrance of Allāh is greater.*[1]

The Prophet, may God bless him and grant him peace, is reported to have said, 'Shall I not inform you of the best of your deeds and the highest in rank and purest in the sight of your Master—a deed which is better than giving gold and silver, and better than to meet your enemies in battle and smite their necks and have your necks smitten by them?' They replied, 'Tell us.' He said, 'The remembrance of *Allāh*.' He also said, as reported by Muᶜādh b. Jabal, 'The son of man can perform no action more likely to save him from God's punishment than the remembrance of *Allāh*.'

For God to 'remember' His servants means that when they invoke His Oneness, he reminds them of Paradise and more besides, as He says, *God rewarded them, on account of what they said, with gardens beneath which flow rivers.*[2] When they invoke Him with his Unique Name—*Allāh*—and call to him with sincerity, He answers them: *If My servants ask you about Me, I am near.*[3] When they invoke Him with gratitude, He increases them: *If you thank Me, I will surely increase you.*[4] Whenever a servant remembers Him, He in return remembers the servant in a compensatory way. When the gnostic remembers Him with his gnosis, He remembers the gnostic by raising the veil that he might see Him. When the believer remembers Him with his faith, He remembers the believer with His mercy and good pleasure. When the repenter remembers Him with repentance, He remembers the repenter with acceptance and forgiveness. When the sinner remembers Him by confessing his sin, He remembers the sinner by concealing him from exposure and pardoning him. When the wicked person remembers Him with wickedness and heedlessness, He remembers the wicked person with punishment and rejection. When the unbeliever remembers Him with unbelief and insolence, He remembers the unbeliever with punishment and requital.

1 Q.XXIX.45.
2 Q.V.85.
3 Q.II.186.
4 Q.XIV.7.

He raises those who laud Him, rectifies those who glorify Him, aids those who praise Him, forgives those who ask His forgiveness, and accepts those who turn back to Him.

۞ ۞ ۞

All the states the servant passes through can be summarised by four states: he is obedient, in which case God remembers him by allowing him to see the blessing of grace which allowed him to be obedient; or he is disobedient, in which case He remembers him by concealing him from exposure and guiding him towards repentance; or he enjoys a blessing, in which case He remembers him by inspiring gratitude in him; or else he suffers a trial, in which case He remembers him by inspiring patience in him.

۞ ۞ ۞

The remembrance of *Allāh* produces five things: God's good pleasure, the softening of the heart, increased goodness, protection from Satan, and abstinence from sin. Those who remember Him can only do so because He remembers them; those who know Him can only do so because He reveals Himself to them; those who declare His Oneness can only do so because He teaches it to them; those who obey Him can only do so because He gives them grace; those who love Him can only do so because He chooses to love them; those who disobey Him can only do so because He forsakes them. Every blessing is His gift, and every trial is His fate; and all things come to pass in due course. A poet said,

> Generous one, I will ever hold to my words,
> And the virtue of Your remembrance is well-remembered.
> Take my hand and guide me to the righteous path,
> For Your guidance is the only true illumination.
> Guide me to an act You love, my only hope;
> Quicken my tongue with remembrance of the Real.

۞ ۞ ۞

Know that the formula of divine Oneness is balanced between negation and affirmation. It begins 'there is no god', which is negation, renunciation, unbelief and atheism, and ends with 'but *Allāh*', which is affirmation, faith, monotheism, submission to God and a testimony of enlightenment. The words 'there is no' negate divinity to all that does not merit it and cannot possess it, and the words 'but *Allāh*' affirm divinity to That which does merit it and must possess it. This is summarised by God's words: *Whosoever disbelieves in idols, and believes in God, has grasped the firmest handle.*[1] For the masses of Muslims (*ʿāma*), the formula 'There is no god but *Allāh*' cleanses their understanding of delusions and vain fancies by affirming Unicity and negating duality. For the spiritual elite (*khāṣa*), it adds strength to their faith and increases their enlightenment by affirming the Essence and the Qualities, and declaring them to be transcendentally beyond the change and blight which affect the qualities of contingent things. For the innermost spiritual elite (*khāṣat al-khāṣa*), it blinds them to their own remembrance [of Him], and affirms for them His grace and blessing, so that their gratitude is ever increasing.

Thus, in *tawḥīd* and the invocation of *tawḥīd*, people are divided into three categories. First there are the masses of Muslims, or those at the beginning stage: theirs in the *tawḥīd* of the tongue, by which they pronounce and invoke, with faith and sincerity, the testimony of *tawḥīd*: 'There is no god but *Allāh*, and Muḥammad is the Messenger of God.' This is submission (*islām*). Secondly there are the elite, or those at the intermediate stage: theirs is the *tawḥīd* of the heart, to which they hold with faith and sincerity. This is faith (*īmān*). Lastly there is the innermost elite: theirs is the *tawḥīd* of the intellect (*ʿaql*), through which they are certain, and through which they witness directly. This is spiritual excellence (*iḥsān*).

✡ ✡ ✡

For those who invoke, then, there are three stations: the invocation

1 Q.II.256.

of the tongue, which is the invocation of the masses of Muslims; the invocation of the heart, which is the invocation of the spiritual elite; and the invocation of the spirit (*rūḥ*), which is the invocation of the innermost elite and the gnostics, who in their extinction (*fanā'*) are unaware of their own invocation and aware only of Him who remembers them and blesses them.

The one who invokes this Unique Name—*Allāh*—passes through several states: the state of passionate love (*walah*) and extinction (*fanā'*), the state of life (*ḥayā*) and subsistence (*baqā'*), and the state of bliss (*niᶜam*) and contentment (*riḍā*).

The first state, that of passionate love and extinction, is experienced by the one who invokes this Name alone and no other at the beginning, making it his confidant, and properly pronouncing the final letter *hā'* of it as he invokes it. The one who does this consistently will be erased on the outside and effaced on the inside. Outwardly, he will appear like a madman, out of his mind with passion, and no one will accept him, and all will avoid him because of the passion that characterises his outward appearance, and the secret of the Name that he invokes. The quality of Godhood is not a quality which anyone can share, and people are unsettled by the one who invokes it, so that he becomes like those of whom God says, *There is no kinship any more between them, nor do they question one another.*[1] Inside, he is virtually dead and extinct, because of the stillness of his essence and his qualities, and his renunciation of his habits and familiar things, and the submission of his body and the piety of his heart. God says of this, *We shall load you with a word of heavy weight,*[2] and, *You see the earth blackened, and then, when We send down water upon it, it quivers and swells, and puts forth herbs of every joyous kind.*[3]

The second state, that of life and subsistence, occurs when the invoker attains realisation of this Name and becomes established in it, so that his qualities and traces are erased, and the spirit of con-

1 Q.XXIII.101.
2 Q.LXXIII.5.
3 Q.XXII.5.

tentment is blown into him after the death of his will and desire. He becomes extinct to his habitual desires and passions, and sheds all his blameworthy attributes, and moves from the state of passionate love and extinction to the state of life and subsistence. He develops a powerful and awesome presence, and all contingent things come to fear and laud him, and humble themselves before him, and seek blessings from him.

The third state, that of bliss and contentment, is experienced by the one who invokes this Name when he lauds God's command, feels compassion for God's creatures, makes no prideful claims about God's religion, expands beyond himself by God and for God, realises the breadth of God's mercy, is no longer affected by God's creations, and is no longer under the thrall of anyone or anything, by God's leave. When he reaches this point, he moves from the state of life and subsistence to the state of bliss and contentment, and lives a life of perpetual bliss and happiness; a life that is sound and peaceful, unsullied by turbidity or change. He gains mastery over his own state, and is given security, tranquillity and stability. He becomes, for his fellow man, like plentiful rain: wherever he goes, things bloom, grow and are nourished. He attains to bliss and contentment in God, and God is content with him. God says, *Thereafter We produced him as another creature. So, blessed be God, the fairest of creators!*[1]

It is said that in a gathering of Shiblī's (God be pleased with him), someone shouted out '*Allāh*!' Shiblī said to him, 'If you are sincere, then you have divulged your secret; and if you are insincere, then you have ruined yourself!'

Similarly, a man once shouted out in the presence of Junayd, God rest his soul, who said to him, 'My brother, if He whom you invoked can see you, and you are present with Him, then you have torn the veil from your intimate seclusion with Him disrespectfully, for the true lover is jealously protective of his beloved. If, on the other hand,

1 Q.xxiii.14.

you invoked Him whilst being absent from him, this amounts to backbiting—and backbiting is forbidden.'

It is said that Abū al-Ḥasan al-Thawrī, God rest his soul, stayed in his house for seven days without eating, drinking or sleeping, repeating '*Allāh, Allāh*'. Abū al-Qāsim al-Junyad was told of this, and said, 'Have the prayer times been maintained?' They answered that Abū al-Ḥasan was offering all his prayers at their proper times, and Junayd said, 'Praise be to God, who has protected him and not allowed Satan to get near him.' He then said to his companions, 'Let us go and visit him, that we might benefit him or he us.' It is said that when al-Junayd went in, he said, 'O Abū al-Ḥasan, when you say *Allāh Allāh*, do you say it through God, or through yourself? If you say it through God, then it is not you who speaks, but it is He speaking on the tongue of His servant, invoking Himself by Himself. But if you are saying it through yourself, then you have only yourself; so what, then, is the meaning of your passion?' Thawrī answered him, 'You are right, teacher!', and his passion subsided.

> I cried out in passion for You when I invoked You,
> For Your mention makes a man moan and die in ardour.
> Whoso loses not his mind in yearning for love,
> Upon my word, lives a miserable life.
> What is remembrance? It is to lose sight
> Of remembrance through passion for the Remembered.
> The one of sound mind has no real remembrance;
> He who moves beyond his remembrance, moves upward.

Know that remembrance (*dhikr*) is to move away from heedlessness (*ghafla*) and forgetfulness (*nisyān*) by means of the permanent presence of the heart and by the faithful repetition of the tongue. The vision of the Master causes the remembrance to flow on the tongue of the servant. It has also been said that remembrance is to exit the sphere of heedlessness for the space of witnessing through fear, ardent love, overwhelming yearning and submission to God. The reality of remembrance is to be fixed solely on the Remembered without being conscious of one's own remembrance, and to be extinct in the act of witnessing without being conscious of one's own witnessing, but only of His; thus one sees the Real, by the Real, and God is the Invoker and the Invoked. Inasmuch as the remembrance is uttered by the tongue of the servant, the servant is the one who remembers; inasmuch as it is He who facilitates this and allows it to proceed from the servant's tongue, He is the One who remembers His servant and facilitates his remembrance; inasmuch as it is He who inspires the thought to begin with, He is the One who remembers Himself on the tongue of His servant. The authentic *ḥadīth* tells us that God says, 'I become his hearing wherewith he hears, his sight wherewith he sees, his tongue wherewith he speaks…'; and another narration has it, 'I become his hearing, sight, tongue, hand and aid.'

✵ ✵ ✵

There are several forms and types of invocation, but the Invoked is One, Indivisible and Infinite. The folk of invocation (*ahl al-dhikr*) are the beloved of the Real, because of what the invocation produces in them. Invocation is of three categories: loud (*jalī*), silent (*khafī*) and true (*ḥaqīqī*). Loud invocation is for beginners. It is uttered by the tongue, and consists of expressions of gratitude, praise, and the magnification of the blessings and favours [of God], and the keeping of covenants. Each instance of it is worth between ten and seventy good deeds.

Silent, inward invocation is for the people of sainthood (*ahl al-wilāya*). It is pronounced secretly in the heart when one has broken free of one's weakness and come to subsist in a state of constant witnessing of the Presence. Each instance of it is worth between seventy and seven hundred good deeds.

True, perfect invocation is for those at the end of the Path (*ahl al-nihāya*). It is the spirit's invocation of the Real's all-seeing Presence with the servant after he has ceased to see his own invocation, whilst subsisting in his external form and life. One instance of it is worth between seven hundred and an infinite number of good deeds. This is because the state of witnessing is an extinction with no pleasure.[1]

The spirit invokes the Essence, the heart invokes the Qualities, and the tongue performs a habitual and outward invocation. If the invocation of the spirit is operative, then the heart ceases to invoke; this is the invocation of the awe of the Essence, which signals that one has reached the level of extinction and nearness. If the invocation of the heart is operative, the tongue falls silent and ceases to invoke; this is the invocation of the blessings and boons of the Qualities, which signals that a remnant of the self remains and extinction has not yet been reached, and that one has not yet been accepted. If the heart's invocation is not operative, then the tongue simply invokes externally, out of habit.

Each of these three invocations is susceptible to a blight. The blight of the spirit's invocation is the intrusion of the inner heart on it. The blight of the heart's invocation is the intrusion of the soul into it. The blight of the soul's invocation is its susceptibility to flaws. The blight of the tongue's invocation is heedlessness and lethargy. A poet said of this,

> He is God, so invoke Him and hymn His praise;
> For none but Him should be glorified.
> In His might, He deserves all praise;
> So can the invocations of his servant encompass Him?
> Were all the seas brought together
> And made into ink, and doubled again,
> And all the trees made pens to write His praise,
> Until they were all spent and used up,
> He would still be called 'the Praised',
> And His creatures would go on praising Him.

1 'An extinction with no pleasure' because it is total extinction in the Real, which necessarily includes the annihilation of the self-awareness required for the experience of pleasure, even the pleasure of the invocation itself.

Now again, as pertains to the invocation, people are divided into three categories. There are the hardworking masses of Muslims, the diligent elite, and the guided innermost elite. The invocation of the masses of Muslims is the starting-point of purification; the invocation of the elite is the midpoint of appreciation; and the invocation of the innermost elite is the endpoint of insight. The invocation of the masses of Muslims is balanced between negation and affirmation; the invocation of the elite is affirmation in affirmation; and the invocation of the innermost elite is the realisation of affirmation's affirmation, without any side-glances or distractions. Those who fear Him invoke Him by His warnings; those who hope in Him invoke Him by His promises; the monotheists invoke Him by His Oneness; those who love Him invoke Him by their vision of Him; the gnostics invoke Him by Him, not by themselves or for themselves. The gnostic invokes God through honouring and magnification; the scholar invokes God through transcendence and glory; the worshipper invokes God through fear and hope; the lover invokes God through passion; the monotheist invokes God through awe and dread; the masses of Muslims invoke God out of mindless habit. The servant is compelled and called to invoke, and has no excuse not to do so as long as he is morally responsible (*mukallaf*).

❁ ❁ ❁

There are three modes of invocation: the beginning is concerned with life and wakefulness, the middle with transcendence and purity, and the end with communion (*waṣla*) and gnosis. The invocation of life and wakefulness, after first fulfilling its conditions, is to repeat often 'O Living, O Sustaining, there is no god but You.' The invocation of purity and transcendence, after first fulfilling its conditions, is to repeat often 'God is my sufficiency, and the best of patrons.'[1]

❁ ❁ ❁

1 Ibn ʿAṭā' Allāh does not give an example for 'communion and gnosis'.

Invocation has three levels: 'heedless invocation', which earns one nothing but ruin and rejection; 'present-minded invocation', by which one attains nearness and increased virtue; and 'totally absorbed invocation', by which one attains love, witnessing and communion. Someone said of this,

> Whenever I invoke You, I am stirred by my thought,
> My mind, and my innermost heart upon Your mention.
> It is as though an emissary of Yours whispers to me:
> 'Beware, heed this reminder, beware!
> Make the vision of your encounter a reminder,
> For the Real reminds you by your encounter.
> Do you not see that the Real's signs are everywhere,
> And that everything points you towards Him?'
> Grant me, then, a pure invocation, and show mercy
> To a servant who perchance keeps You in his heart.

❁ ❁ ❁

Know that invocation is always one of three: it is either invocation of the tongue, which is to knock upon the door of the King, and is an expiation for sins and a means of ascending degrees; or it is invocation of the heart, which is to be granted permission to address the King, and is a means of drawing closer to Him; or it is invocation of the spirit, which is to speak and converse with the King, and to be present with Him and to witness Him.

Invocation of the tongue with an oblivious heart is mere habitual invocation, devoid of any hope of going further. Invocation of the tongue with presence of heart is worshipful invocation, from which benefit may come. Invocation with all of the tongue and a full heart is the way of unveiling and witnessing, and no one but God knows its worth.

It has been said, 'Whoever begins his spiritual journey by reciting *sūrat al-Ikhlāṣ* often, God will illuminate his heart and strengthen his *tawḥīd*.'

Bazzār narrates on the authority of Anas b. Mālik that the

Prophet, may God bless him and grant him peace, said, 'Whoso recites *Say: He, Allāh, is One*[1] one hundred thousand times, purchases his own soul from God Almighty, and a herald from God Almighty calls out in His heavens and His earth, "Yea, so-and-so has been freed by God! Anyone who is owed anything by him should seek it from God Almighty."'

It has also been said, 'When a person repeats many entreaties for forgiveness, God gives life to his heart, makes his provision plentiful, forgives his sins, provides for him in a way he does not expect, gives him a way out of every dire strait, and bends the things of this world to his will. Everything has a penalty, and the penalty of the gnostic is to lose presence of mind in invocation.'

An authentic *ḥadīth* tells us that the Prophet, may God bless him and grant him peace, said, 'Everything has a polish, and the polish of the heart is the invocation of God, and the best invocation is *there is no god but Allāh.*' The way to polish, shine and illuminate the heart is with invocation and meditation. The best and noblest of gatherings are those which are accompanied by meditation on *tawḥīd*. Trust (*tawakkul*) is the act of the heart, and *tawḥīd* is the speech of the heart. The door to invocation is meditation (*fikr*); the door to meditation is wakefulness (*yaqaẓa*); the door to wakefulness is detachment (*zuhd*); the door to detachment is contentment (*qanāʿa*); the door to contentment is concern for the Hereafter; the door to concern for the Hereafter is piety (*taqwā*); the door to piety is this world (*dunyā*);[2] the door to this world is desire (*hawā*); the door to desire is avarice (*ḥirṣ*); the door to avarice is hope (*amal*); and hope is the fatal disease which never heals. The root of hope is love for this world; the door to love for this world is heedlessness; and heedlessness is a cover which veils the innermost heart. *Tawḥīd* is the elixir which protects from all harm, as is said, 'By the Name of *Allāh*, with whose Name nothing can cause harm on earth or in the sky; and He is the All-Hearing,

1 Q.CXII.1-4.
2 'The door to piety is this world' means that piety is only attained in the world; the world is the venue for piety, the place where free will is exercised for good or ill.

the All-Knowing.' The greater part of *tawḥīd*, and its core, heart and essence, is the *tawḥīd* of this Unique Name, and its uniqueness, and the gnosis it imparts.

It is said that a great gnostic was asked about the Supreme Name of God, he answered, 'It is to say *Allāh* without being there yourself.' This is because when a created being says *Allāh*, he says it with his ego; yet mystical realities cannot be perceived by the ego. The one who says *Allāh* by pronouncing the letters of the word has not really said *Allāh*, or really invoked it, because it is far beyond ego, letters, human understanding, physical form, shape, imagination and fancy. Nevertheless, our Lord in His grace accepts this from us, and rewards us for it, because there are no other means by which human beings can invoke Him and declare His Oneness.

Yet, because of how He favours and cares for the gnostics and those endowed with spiritual knowledge and mastery, He is not content to leave them to their own invocation of Him, as He says, *There is not one of us, save that he has a known station.*[1] When someone says *Allāh* and invokes the Name, he does so by God's grace, aid and favour, not by his own power; and in doing so, all the divine Names are realised for him, and his invocation of the Name becomes for him like the divine 'Be!' (*kun*), which brings things into being, so that all things seem to him engendered by this invocation. The one who says *Allāh* for the sake of pure truth, not for any other goal but purely out of knowledge, gnosis and reverence, acknowledging the divine Transcendence and Majesty and bearing witness to it, has truly exalted God, invoked Him, magnified Him, and recognised His glory. Their invocation of God and declaration of His Oneness is a manifestation of His contentment with them in that He gives them the grace to do so as befits Him. Gnosis is vision, not knowledge; direct sight, not second-hand information; witnessing, not description; discovery, not veiling. They are not who they are; they are no longer what they were. He says, *He is naught but a servant whom We*

1 Q.xxxvii.164.

have favoured;[1] 'And if I love him, I become his hearing, sight, hand, and aid.'

> How to reach Him, when He is transcendent,
> And does not dwell in any place?
> Their being is annihilated in His Being,
> Beyond all substance, above all accident.
> Nothing resembles Him, so 'Where?', and 'How',
> And 'When?' are questions devoid of meaning.
> What a wonder, that He is both
> As clear as can be, and utterly hidden.

❁ ❁ ❁

In reality, no one invokes God but God, and no one knows Him but He, and no one truly affirms His Oneness but He. Regarding His invocation of Himself, consider His words, *The remembrance of Allāh is greater*,[2] which means that His remembrance of Himself is greater, mightier and more perfect than anyone else's remembrance of Him. Regarding His knowledge, consider His words, *They do not esteem Allāh as He ought to be esteemed*,[3] which means that He alone knows the perfection of His Essence and the magnificence of His Qualities, while His creatures are unable even to gain full knowledge of one another, never mind of any of His Qualities. Regarding His affirmation of His Oneness, consider His words, *Allāh bears witness that there is no god but He*,[4] which means that He alone has perfect and true knowledge of His own Oneness, and His creations could only declare His Oneness after He declared it Himself. He spreads some of its light to His angels and the people of knowledge, according to what each is able to bear, and what was ordained for them in His knowledge before time began. Their knowledge exists by the light of His *tawḥīd* [of Himself], and not by His *tawḥīd* itself. No gnostic

1 Q.XLIII.59.
2 Q.XXIX.45.
3 Q.VI.91.
4 Q.III.18.

is able to know Him [except through what He reveals to them]; they possess knowledge because it is latent in them but this is the farthest extent they can reach, and this latent knowledge is like the light of a lamp compared to the light of the sun as it casts its rays upon it. Thus, the *tawḥīd* that is most firmly rooted in the intellect, understood in the mind and united with the heart is the one that a person attains through witnessing what is latent in his own soul after examining it wisely and critically, so that his intellect perceives it first-hand rather than by rote learning, doubt, supposition or confusion. *Tawḥīd* learned by rote is of little value or benefit, because it means to adopt the belief of another without knowing the reasoning or evidence behind it, and none are content with such but the foolhardy, the coarse, the dull-witted, the ignorant and the ignoble. Such folk are distant and veiled from God, and this is true depravity—may God protect us and you from being so veiled, and make us people of knowledge, understanding, certitude and gnosis, by His grace!

۞ ۞ ۞

Abū Saʿīd al-Khudrī related that the Prophet, may God bless him and give him peace, said, 'There are four kinds of hearts: an empty heart wherein is a shining lamp, which is the heart of a believer; an upturned black heart, which is the heart of an unbeliever; a sealed heart tied shut, which is the heart of a hypocrite; and a heart wherein faith and hypocrisy are mixed—the faith in it is like a plant nourished with goodly water, and the hypocrisy in it is like a blister nourished by pus. Whichever of the two substances is more abundant will determine this heart's nature.' Another narration has, 'will claim it'.

ʿAlī, may God ennoble his countenance and be pleased with him, said, 'The empty heart is empty because of the person's asceticism in this world and his withdrawal from base desires, and its shining lamp is the light of certitude by which it sees.'

Someone else said that the empty heart is the one absorbed with *tawḥīd* and empty of doubts, misgivings and rote learning, and withdrawn from everything but God. The upturned heart is the heart of a person who chooses caprice as his god, so that God turned him away from knowledge, and because it was upended it saw the darkness of idolatry instead of the light of *tawḥīd*.

One of the gnostics said of this, 'The blackest darkness is the darkness of knowledge,[1] and the worst ignorance is the ignorance of rote learning.'

The sealed heart is the one that is veiled by the darkness of ignorant rote learning from beholding the sun of prophethood and *tawḥīd*. God says, *They say, 'We found our fathers on a path, and we shall be guided by their footsteps.' Thus it is that whenever We sent a warner to a town before you, the folk who lived in luxury there would say, 'We found our fathers on a path, and we shall follow in their footsteps'*;[2] *When they are told to follow what God has revealed, they say, 'Nay, we shall follow what we found our fathers doing'*.[3]

The mixed heart is the heart of the one who is caught between his soul's passions and his recognised duties, although he does fulfil them outwardly. Ostentation (*riyā'*)[4] is idolatry, and idolatry renders good deeds worthless; and the worst kind of ostentation is ostentation about faith. God says, *There are those whose words would please you in this life, yet Allāh sees what is in their hearts, and in truth they are the bitterest rivals*;[5] *They do not go to pray except lazily*;[6] *Woe unto those who pray and are heedless of their prayers; those who make a show, and refuse small*

1 What is intended here is dry scholastic learning which, as Sufis have often been at pains to stress, can potentially veil the aspirant if it is taken as an end rather than as a means and pursued to the exclusion of gnosis. It is not that knowledge itself is the 'blackest darkness', but that the darkness of knowledge that brings no benefit is all the darker for being confused for light.

2 Q.XLIII.22–23.

3 Q.XXXI.21.

4 By 'ostentation' here Ibn ʿAṭā' Allāh means 'hypocrisy' or an 'active' form of hypocrisy.

5 Q.II.204.

6 Q.IX.54.

kindnesses.[1] In summary, whatever is in the heart, this is undoubtedly what is affirmed.[2]

Some have said that the heart and the power of its light, *tawḥīd* and brightness is akin to a lamp: the candle is the heart, the water is the intellect, and the oil is knowledge, which is the spirit of the lamp, and the spirit of certitude will be stronger the more knowledge there is: *He aided them with a spirit from Him* (Q.LVIII.22). Then the wick is faith, which is the foundation and the means by which the light spreads.

So, the purity of the candle, which is the sincere heart, displays the colour of the water, which is the aided intellect; and the purity, fineness and abundance of the oil, which is knowledge, allows the light to shine forth, which is faith; and the strength and quality of the wick determines the strength of the certitude, which is like faith in its power, which is drawn from asceticism, fear and reverence. The brightness of the fire illuminates the soul, which is like knowledge in the elements of consciousness, piety, gnosis, and resistance of caprice and instinctive desires. Therefore, knowledge is the source of *tawḥīd*, and the person who is affirming *tawḥīd* possesses it to the extent of his possession of the source [knowledge]. Trust is the heart's deed, and *tawḥīd* is its speech. The highest and noblest activity is to meditate on *tawḥīd*; and as the heart broadens with knowledge, it detaches from this world and loses its caprice, desire and ambition for it, and its faith grows, and its *tawḥīd* is perfected.

Others have said that the heart is like a throne and the breast like a footstool: when the breast broadens through knowledge of faith and expands through the light of certitude, it becomes a footstool whose knowledge covers the outward world of dominion and the inward world of domination, both in itself and outside itself. The person with such a heart becomes enveloped with gnosis and proceeds on the spiritual journey adorned with the character of the

1 Q.CVII.4-7.
2 That is, whether it inclines more to faith or to hypocrisy.

Supreme Assembly of angels, even as the *ḥadīth* says, 'My servant continues to draw nearer to me with voluntary acts until I love him, and when I love him, I become his hearing wherewith he hears,' and so on. When his heart fills with *tawḥīd*, it becomes like a throne, and its substance shrugs off the lower human traits and is adorned with the attributes of the Supreme Assembly of angels, and its gnosis rises to the lower assembly of angels, and its insight is perfected by the light of the Name of the Essence, and its status becomes like that of the divine Throne above all creatures. It adorns itself with the attributes of God, and the Most Beautiful Names become its qualities and its nature. It achieves realisation and true insight, and goes beyond the invocation to become annihilated in the Invoked. It conveys God's mercy to his fellow man, and calls to Truth by Truth. For God has said, 'Neither My Throne nor My Footstool can contain Me, but the heart of My servant can.' That is, it can contain Him through *tawḥīd*, faith, knowledge, gnosis, certitude, love and sincerity, which are a grace and favour from God, who cannot be contained by any place, any imagination, any locus, any physical space, nor any natural law.

۞ ۞ ۞

The affirmation of God's transcendence is of three categories: that of the masses of Muslims, that of the elite, and that of the elite among the elite.

The masses of Muslims affirm His transcendence above any defects, and cleanse their hearts from any notions that He could have a partner, opposite or equal, or that divinity could be anything other than His alone.

The elite affirm His transcendence beyond any limit on His praises, for the praise of the Eternal must be infinite, and it is impossible to limit the infinite. They cleanse their hearts of heedlessness and languor by remaining in a state of invocation and reverence, and of constant recognition of His graces and favours.

The elite among the elite affirm His transcendence by ridding themselves of any acknowledgement of their own souls even as they do so, and paying no regard to their own humanity, and cleansing themselves of any claim to active agency in the matter; that is, the intellect does not observe itself in the act of affirming His transcendence.

۞ ۞ ۞

Gnosis of God is also of three kinds. First there is gnosis of Oneness, which is imparted by the voice of *tawḥīd* through the proofs of perfection and eternality. Secondly there is gnosis of Power, which is attained through the hard work of self-purification and spiritual excellence, through the proofs of grace and favour. Thirdly there is gnosis of Love, which is attained through unveilings and direct witnessing of the divine manifestation, through the proofs of generosity and largesse.

۞ ۞ ۞

The learned folk (*ʿulamāʾ*) who have spoken about knowledge of God are likewise divided into three groups. There are those who say, 'There is nothing in existence that does not know God.' Then there are those who say, 'There is nothing in existence that *does* know God.' Then there are those who say, 'No one knows God but God.'

Those who hold that everything in existence knows God are speaking on the level of the divine Names and Qualities. The first obligation in religious study is to recognise God for what He is by reflecting on His Essence and Acts, and deducing the existence of the Creator from His creation and the Doer from His deed, for the intellect is compelled to recognise the existence of the Doer because it knows that it is impossible for any deed to exist without a doer. God says, *Is there any doubt in Allāh, the Maker of heaven and earth?*;[1] *Allāh bears witness that there is no god but He.*[2] Consider also the *ḥadīth* of Muʿādh b. Jabal when the Messenger of God, may God bless him

1 Q.XIV.10.
2 Q.III.18.

and give him peace, sent him to Yemen and said, 'You are going to folk who are People of the Book, so let the first thing to which you invite them be worship of God. If they recognise God, then tell them that God has commanded them to pray five prayers.'[1] So God[2] and His Messenger[3] affirmed that they do know of God, and denied that they have any reason to doubt in His existence. God says, *Were you to ask them who created them, they would say, 'Allāh.' Why, then, are they diverted?*;[4] *Were you to ask them who created the heavens and the earth, they would say, 'The Almighty, the All-Knowing'.*[5] These verses refer in general to asking creation about their Creator. Thus, both logic and revelation affirm that there is nothing in existence that can doubt the existence of the Maker, the Doer, the Chooser, nor anyone who is ignorant of His Name.

As for those who say that nothing in the world can know God, they are referring to a knowledge that encompasses the true reality of His Essence and Qualities as they really are, and according to their exact nature. It is an obvious truth that a limited contingent being cannot have encompassing knowledge of the One Absolute Eternal Being, because that would amount to the encompassment of the object [of knowledge] by its subject, which is rationally impossible. God says, *They cannot encompass any knowledge of His, unless He wills it*;[6] *They cannot encompass Him with knowledge*;[7] *They do not esteem Allāh as He ought to be esteemed*;[8] that is, they do not truly know Him. The Prophet, may God bless him and give him peace, said, 'If you

1 A slightly different version of this *ḥadīth* appeared earlier: 'You are going to people who follow the Book, so let the first thing to which you invite them be worship of God. If they acknowledge God, tell them that God has charged them with certain obligations.'
2 In the above Qur'ānic verses.
3 In the *ḥadīth* of Muʿādh.
4 Q.xliii.87.
5 Q.xliii.9.
6 Q.ii.255.
7 Q.xx.110.
8 Q.vi.91.

truly knew God, you would walk upon the oceans, and the mountains would move at your command.' And he said, 'If you truly knew God, you would attain that knowledge after which there can be no ignorance; yet no one has ever done so.' They said, 'Not even you, Messenger of God?' He replied, 'Not even I.' They said, 'We did not realise that even the Messengers fall short of this.' God is too Mighty and Glorious for anyone to know everything about Him; this knowledge is impossible for creation, but necessary for God, because he knows Himself, His Qualities and everything else about Himself exactly as it is, absolutely and without limit, and this encompassment cannot be attained by anyone else.

As for those who say that only God can know God, again they are referring to absolute, encompassing knowledge. He is the Creator of all things, the Originator of all contingent beings, the Director of their affairs, the Knower of their fate and their extent, the One who gives them being and takes it away, the One who begins them and returns them. God says, *Allāh is the Creator of all things, and He is the Guardian of all things;*[1] *Such is Allāh, your Lord, the Creator of all things; there is no god but He. Why, then, are you diverted?;*[2] *Is there another creator besides Allāh?;*[3] *Allāh encompasses all things with knowledge;*[4] *He keeps count of all things;*[5] *Allāh has power over all things;*[6] *He ordains the matter from heaven to earth, and then it shall rise up to Him on a day as long as a thousand years in your reckoning;*[7] *The angels and the Spirit shall rise up to Him on a day as long as fifty thousand years.*[8] The Messenger of God, may God bless him and give him peace, said, 'I cannot praise You enough; You are as You have praised Yourself.' God commanded him to say,

1 Q.xxxix.62.
2 Q.xl.62.
3 Q.xxxv.3.
4 Q.lxv.12.
5 Q.lxxii.28.
6 Q.ii.20.
7 Q.xxxii.5.
8 Q.lxx.4.

Had I knowledge of the unseen, I could have amassed a great many treasures.[1] He was the best of all creation, the leader of the world, the axis of existence, the spirit of all created things, but he acknowledged his limits in the face of the Infinite. This was due to his perfect gnosis, vast knowledge and exalted status—may God bless him and give him peace, with a blessing that pleases him and increases him in nobility, glory, exception, and ever-growing nearness to his Lord.

So, it is established by both reason and revelation that none of God's creatures can know God as He truly is, and no one knows Him as He is worthy of being known except for Him. A poet said,

> You spoke without speaking, for such do you speak;
> You may speak with words, or communicate without them.
> You appeared to me when before You had been hidden,
> And showed me a flash of lighting, and made it speak to me.
> For my part, what else could I say but that I
> Was a pauper with nothing to offer the Truth;
> I was ignorant, unknowing; I gestured but said nothing;
> I became a slave to Him, and who on earth would free me?
> I became extinct to myself through Him, and disappeared in Him,
> If He wills, He will annihilate me or preserve me.
> No one knows God but God himself,
> And those who confess ignorance of Him speak truly.

Know that the people are divided into three categories with regard to how they invoke their *tawḥīd*. First there are the masses of Muslims and the people at the beginning of the path, who invoke with the tongue with speech and words affirming the testimony of faith, which is submission to God (*islām*).[2] Then there are the elite or the people midway on the path, who invoke with the heart with belief, conviction, trust and sincerity, which is faith (*īmān*). Then there are the elite

1 Q.VII.188.

2 Here, towards the end of the treatise, Ibn ʿAṭā' Allāh returns to the three concepts of *islām*, *īmān* and *iḥsān* discussed at the beginning of the work and at intervals throughout.

among the elite, or those at the end of the path, who invoke with the intellect with direct perception, certitude, and innate witnessing, which is spiritual excellence (*iḥsān*). The different levels of people's knowledge and *tawḥīd*—be they among the elites or the masses—concerns their knowledge of the totality or the distinct nature of the Names and Qualities, but not knowledge of the Essence. This is because the basis of knowledge is 'knowledge of truth' (*maʿrifat ḥaqq*), and 'knowledge of reality' (*maʿrifat ḥaqīqa*), and 'knowledge of reality' in this case would mean knowledge of the Essence, which no one can attain because it is impossible. To accept that there are things one simply cannot know is itself knowledge; while seeking after knowledge of the nature of the Essence is setting oneself up as a god![1] God says, *They cannot encompass Him in knowledge.*[2] Abū Bakr al-Ṣiddīq, may God be well pleased with him, said, 'Glory be to Him who has not made any path to knowing Him, save for the inability to know him.'

As for knowledge of truth, this means knowledge of the Names and Qualities, which is available to humanity, and those who have knowledge of it occupy different ranks. Some look at His actions and recognise them as His actions and creations, and this is the limit of their knowledge and what their minds can perceive, and they go no further. Then there are those who perceive the power of the All-Powerful and observe His Qualities and discern His Wisdom, and the Acts do not veil them from the Qualities. This is the limit of their knowledge and what their minds can perceive, and they go no further. Then there are those who look to the Creator, not the creation, and the Qualities do not veil them from the glory of the Essence. This is the limit of perception and the farthest reach of the intellect beyond which it cannot go. This is the limit of the knowledge that begins with perceiving the Creator through the creation, as God says,

1 As Ibn ʿAṭā' Allāh has earlier explained, knowledge can only be of the Names and Qualities and not of the Essence. To assume to seek knowledge of the Essence is to set oneself up as equal to God.

2 Q.XX.110.

Say, 'Behold what is in the heavens and the earth…';[1] *Will they not behold the camel, and how it was created?;*[2] *Truly in the creation of the heavens and the earth, and the alternation of night and day, and the ships that sail upon the ocean, are signs;*[3] *In the earth are signs for those with sure faith; and in your own selves—will you not see?.*[4] This knowledge then culminates with perceiving the creation through the Creator, as God says, *Does it not suffice to your Lord that He is witness of all things?;*[5] *Is there any doubt in Allāh, the Maker of heaven and earth?*[6]

People are also divided into three categories when it comes to beholding (*mushāhada*): the beginning is for the masses of Muslims, the middle for the elite, and the end for the elite among the elite. The masses of Muslims behold the beauty of the perfection of spiritual realities as they are manifested in their most accessible material forms. The elite behold the beauty of the perfection of the archetypes of the spiritual realities that are manifested in perishable forms. The elite among the elite behold the beauty of the majesty of Supreme Transcendent Absolute Beauty manifested in existence and which the mystery of the Most Beautiful Names prolongs. Every act of beholding is commensurate to how far the veil has been drawn back, and to whatever was decreed for a person to behold in the Mother of the Book where fate is decreed. One person beholds a created being with a specific identity, perceiving one creature through another. Another person beholds an absolute reality, perceiving one truth through another. What a difference there is between a considerate beholder and an oblivious one! A poet said of this,

1 Q.x.101.
2 Q.lxxxviii.17.
3 Q.ii.164.
4 Q.li.20-21.
5 Q.xli.53.
6 Q.xiv.10.

He appears with the attributes of beauty,
So that nothing ugly or base can be seen.
When He showed Himself to me in all I saw,
And manifested the truth to me in every view,
I no longer presumptuously restricted beauty,
And I beheld the secrets of beauty without limits.
In every sight, my heart beholds Him;
In every sound, it hears a holy hymn.
All that I hear is now sacred music;
How could I put a limit on such melodies?
I see them all through the qualities of Beauty,
Like a gift that is precious, whether ignored or cherished.

Take heed—may God have mercy on you—of these beautiful mysteries and teachings, and meditate on them and understand the meanings of the secrets, and you will see wondrous things and benefit greatly. Pray for the one who wrote them, and for all who copy them, that God might benefit them all with their teachings and knowledge. We ask Him to illuminate our insights with the light of His *tawḥīd* and His gnosis, and to nourish our intellects with His grace and guidance, and to guard our beliefs with adherence to His Book and Tradition. He is the Guide to the path, who shows the seeker the way to realisation; the Helper and Aider, the One who presents a cup of fresh water from the wellspring of gnosis and subtle mysteries to whomever of His servants He will, by His grace, favour and kindness. He is my Sufficiency and my Patron on the path to expanding my breast and illuminating my heart. The command rests with God, and there is no power save with God.

Here ends *The Pure Intention: On Knowledge of the Unique Name Allāh*, an explanation of the meanings of its secrets and the benefits of invoking it, and how to expose oneself to the radiance of its illuminations. Praise be to God, and thanks be to Him for all His favours, first and last. May blessings and peace be upon our master

Muḥammad and his family, outwardly and inwardly, and my God be pleased with his successors, companions, wives, progeny, those who followed them, and all those of his community and his faith who follow them with sincerity until the Day of Resurrection.